MANHATTAN PREP

Geometry

GRE® Strategy Guide

This volume guides students through the intricacies of shapes, planes, lines, angles, and objects, illustrating every geometric principle, formula, and problem type tested on the GRE.

guide **3**

Geometry GRE Strategy Guide, Fourth Edition

10-digit International Standard Book Number: 1-937707-85-7
13-digit International Standard Book Number: 978-1-937707-85-9
eISBN: 978-1-941234-15-0

Note: *GRE, Graduate Record Exam, Educational Testing Service,* and *ETS* are all registered trademarks of the Educational Testing Service, which neither sponsors nor is affiliated in any way with this product.

Layout Design: Dan McNaney and Cathy Huang
Cover Design: Dan McNaney and Frank Callaghan
Cover Photography: Amy Pierce

INSTRUCTIONAL GUIDE SERIES

SUPPLEMENTAL MATERIALS

June 3rd, 2014

Dear Student,

Thank you for picking up a copy of GRE *Geometry*. I hope this book provides just the guidance you need to get the most out of your GRE studies.

As with most accomplishments, there were many people involved in the creation of the book you are holding. First and foremost is Zeke Vanderhoek, the founder of Manhattan Prep. Zeke was a lone tutor in New York when he started the company in 2000. Now, 14 years later, the company has instructors and offices nationwide and contributes to the studies and successes of thousands of GRE, GMAT, LSAT, and SAT students each year.

Our Manhattan Prep Strategy Guides are based on the continuing experiences of our instructors and students. We are particularly indebted to our instructors Stacey Koprince, Dave Mahler, Liz Ghini Moliski, Emily Meredith Sledge, and Tommy Wallach for their hard work on this edition. Dan McNaney and Cathy Huang provided their design expertise to make the books as user-friendly as possible, and Liz Krisher made sure all the moving pieces came together at just the right time. Beyond providing additions and edits for this book, Chris Ryan and Noah Teitelbaum continue to be the driving force behind all of our curriculum efforts. Their leadership is invaluable. Finally, thank you to all of the Manhattan Prep students who have provided input and feedback over the years. This book wouldn't be half of what it is without your voice.

At Manhattan Prep, we continually aspire to provide the best instructors and resources possible. We hope that you will find our commitment manifest in this book. If you have any questions or comments, please email me at dgonzalez@manhattanprep.com. I'll look forward to reading your comments, and I'll be sure to pass them along to our curriculum team.

Thanks again, and best of luck preparing for the GRE!

Sincerely,

Dan Gonzalez
President
Manhattan Prep

HOW TO ACCESS YOUR ONLINE RESOURCES

If you...

⊗ **are a registered Manhattan Prep GRE® student**

and have received this book as part of your course materials, you have AUTOMATIC access to ALL of our online resources. This includes all practice exams, question banks, and online updates to this book. To access these resources, follow the instructions in the Welcome Guide provided to you at the start of your program. Do NOT follow the instructions below.

⊗ **purchased this book from the Manhattan Prep online store or at one of our centers**

1. Go to: www.manhattanprep.com/gre/studentcenter.

2. Log in using the username and password used when your account was set up.

⊗ **purchased this book at a retail location**

1. Create an account with Manhattan Prep at the website: www.manhattanprep.com/gre/createaccount.

2. Go to: www.manhattanprep.com/gre/access.

3. Follow the instructions on the screen.

Your online access begins on the day that you register your book at the above URL.

You only need to register your product ONCE at the above URL. To use your online resources any time AFTER you have completed the registration process, log in to the following URL: www.manhattanprep.com/gre/studentcenter.

Please note that online access is nontransferable. This means that only NEW and UNREGISTERED copies of the book will grant you online access. Previously used books will NOT provide any online resources.

⊗ **purchased an eBook version of this book**

1. Create an account with Manhattan Prep at the website: www.manhattanprep.com/gre/createaccount.

2. Email a copy of your purchase receipt to gre@manhattanprep.com to activate your resources. Please be sure to use the same email address to create an account that you used to purchase the eBook.

For any technical issues, email techsupport@manhattanprep.com or call 800-576-4628.

TABLE *of* CONTENTS

guide 3

Chapter 1
of Geometry

Introduction

In This Chapter...

The Revised GRE

Question Formats in Detail

Chapter 1

Introduction

We know that you're looking to succeed on the GRE so that you can go to graduate school and do the things you want to do in life.

We also know that you may not have done math since high school, and that you may never have learned words like "adumbrate" or "sangfroid." We know that it's going to take hard work on your part to get a top GRE score, and that's why we've put together the only set of books that will take you from the basics all the way up to the material you need to master for a near-perfect score, or whatever your goal score may be. You've taken the first step. Now it's time to get to work!

How to Use These Materials

Manhattan Prep's GRE materials are comprehensive. But keep in mind that, depending on your score goal, it may not be necessary to get absolutely everything. Grad schools only see your overall Quantitative, Verbal, and Writing scores—they don't see exactly which strengths and weaknesses went into creating those scores.

You may be enrolled in one of our courses, in which case you already have a syllabus telling you in what order you should approach the books. But if you bought this book online or at a bookstore, feel free to approach the books—and even the chapters within the books—in whatever order works best for you. For the most part, the books, and the chapters within them, are independent; you don't have to master one section before moving on to the next. So if you're having a hard time with something in particular, you can make a note to come back to it later and move on to another section. Similarly, it may not be necessary to solve every single practice problem for every section. As you go through the material, continually assess whether you understand and can apply the principles in each individual section and chapter. The best way to do this is to solve the Check Your Skills and Practice Sets throughout. If you're confident you have a concept or method down, feel free to move on. If you struggle with something, make note of it for further review. Stay active in your learning and stay oriented toward the test—it's easy to read something and think you understand it, only to have trouble applying it in the 1–2 minutes you have to solve a problem.

Study Skills

As you're studying for the GRE, try to integrate your learning into your everyday life. For example, vocabulary is a big part of the GRE, as well as something you just can't "cram" for—you're going to want to do at least a little bit of vocab every day. So try to learn and internalize a little bit at a time, switching up topics often to help keep things interesting.

Keep in mind that, while many of your study materials are on paper (including Education Testing Service's [ETS's] most recent source of official GRE questions, *The Official Guide to the GRE revised General Test, Second Edition*), your exam will be administered on a computer. Because this is a computer-based test, you will *not* be able to underline portions of reading passages, write on diagrams of geometry figures, or otherwise physically mark up problems. So get used to this now. Solve the problems in these books on scratch paper. (Each of our books talks specifically about what to write down for different problem types.)

Again, as you study, stay focused on the test-day experience. As you progress, work on timed drills and sets of questions. Eventually, you should be taking full practice tests (available at www.manhattanprep.com/gre) under actual timed conditions.

The Revised GRE

As of August 1, 2011, the Quantitative and Verbal sections of the GRE underwent a number of changes. The actual body of knowledge being tested is more or less the same as it ever was, but the *way* that knowledge is tested changed. Here's a brief summary of the changes, followed by a more comprehensive assessment of the new exam.

The current test is a little longer than the old test, lengthened from about 3.5 hours to about 4 hours. When you sign up for the exam at www.ets.org/gre, you will be told to plan to be at the center for 5 hours, since there will be some paperwork to complete when you arrive, and occasionally test-takers are made to wait a bit before being allowed to begin.

Taking a four-hour exam can be quite exhausting, so it's important to practice not only out of these books, but also on full-length computer-based practice exams, such as the six such exams you have gained access to by purchasing this book (see page 7 for details).

There are now two scored Math sections and two scored Verbal sections. A new score scale of 130–170 is used in place of the old 200–800 scale. More on this later.

The Verbal section of the GRE changed dramatically. The Antonyms and Analogies disappeared. The Text Completion and Reading Comprehension remain, expanded and remixed in a few new ways. Vocabulary is still important, but is tested only in the context of complete sentences.

The Quant section of the new GRE still contains the same multiple-choice problems, Quantitative Comparisons, and Data Interpretations (which are really a subset of multiple-choice problems). The revised test also contains two new problem formats, which we will introduce in this section.

On both Verbal and Quant, some of the new question types have more than one correct answer, or otherwise break out of the mold of traditional multiple-choice exams. You might say that computer-based exams are finally taking advantage of the features of computers.

One way that this is true is that the new exam includes a small, on-screen, four-function calculator with a square root button. Many test-takers will rejoice at the advent of this calculator. It is true that the GRE calculator will reduce emphasis on computation—but look out for problems, such as percents questions with tricky wording, that are likely to foil those who rely on the calculator too much. *In short, the calculator may make your life a bit easier from time to time, but it's not a game changer.* There are **zero** questions that can be solved *entirely* with a calculator. You will still need to know the principles contained in the six Quant books (of the eight-book Manhattan Prep GRE series).

Finally, don't worry about whether the new GRE is harder or easier than the old GRE. You are being judged against other test-takers, all of whom are in the same boat. So if the new formats are harder, they are harder for other test-takers as well.

Additionally, graduate schools to which you will be applying have been provided with conversion charts so that applicants with old and new GRE scores can be compared fairly (GRE scores are valid for five years).

Exam Structure

The revised test has six sections. You will get a 10-minute break between the third and fourth sections and a 1-minute break between the others. The Analytical Writing section is always first. The other five sections can be seen in any order and will include:

- Two Verbal Reasoning sections (20 questions each in 30 minutes per section)
- Two Quantitative Reasoning sections (20 questions each in 35 minutes per section)
- Either an unscored section or a research section

An unscored section will look just like a third Verbal or Quantitative Reasoning section, and you will not be told which of them doesn't count. If you get a research section, it will be identified as such, and will be the last section you get.

Section #	Section Type	# Questions	Time	Scored?
1	Analytical Writing	2 essays	30 minutes each	Yes
2	Verbal #1	Approx. 20	30 minutes	Yes
3	Quantitative #1 *(order can vary)*	Approx. 20	35 minutes	Yes
10-Minute Break				
4	Verbal #2	Approx. 20	30 minutes	Yes
5	Quantitative #2 *(order can vary)*	Approx. 20	35 minutes	Yes
?	Unscored Section *(Verbal or Quant, order can vary)*	Approx. 20	30 or 35 minutes	No
Last	Research Section	Varies	Varies	No

All the question formats will be looked at in detail later in the chapter.

Using the Calculator

The addition of a small, four-function calculator with a square root button means that re-memorizing times tables or square roots is less important than it used to be. However, the calculator is not a cure-all; in many problems, the difficulty is in figuring out what numbers to put into the calculator in the first place. In some cases, using a calculator will actually be less helpful than doing the problem some other way. Take a look at an example:

> If x is the remainder when (11)(7) is divided by 4 and y is the remainder when (14)(6) is divided by 13, what is the value of $x + y$?

Solution: This problem is designed so that the calculator won't tell the whole story. Certainly, the calculator will tell you that $11 \times 7 = 77$. When you divide 77 by 4, however, the calculator yields an answer of 19.25. The remainder is not 0.25 (a remainder is always a whole number).

You might just go back to your pencil and paper, and find the largest multiple of 4 that is less than 77. Since 4 does go into 76, you can conclude that 4 would leave a remainder of 1 when dividing into 77.

MANHATTAN
PREP

1

(Notice that you don't even need to know how many times 4 goes into 76, just that it goes in. One way to mentally "jump" to 76 is to say, 4 goes into 40, so it goes into 80…that's a bit too big, so take away 4 to get 76.)

However, it is also possible to use the calculator to find a remainder. Divide 77 by 4 to get 19.25. Thus, 4 goes into 77 nineteen times, with a remainder left over. Now use your calculator to multiply 19 (JUST 19, not 19.25) by 4. You will get 76. The remainder is $77 - 76$, which is 1. Therefore, $x = 1$. You could also multiply the leftover 0.25 times 4 (the divisor) to find the remainder of 1.

Use the same technique to find y. Multiply 14 by 6 to get 84. Divide 84 by 13 to get 6.46. Ignore everything after the decimal, and just multiply 6 by 13 to get 78. The remainder is therefore $84 - 78$, which is 6. Therefore, $y = 6$.

Since you are looking for $x + y$, and $1 + 6 = 7$, the answer is 7.

You can see that blind faith in the calculator can be dangerous. Use it responsibly! And this leads us to…

Practice Using the Calculator!

On the revised GRE, the on-screen calculator will slow you down or lead to incorrect answers if you're not careful! If you plan to use it on test day (which you should), you'll want to practice first.

We have created an online practice calculator for you to use. To access this calculator, go to www.manhattanprep.com/gre and sign in to the student center using the instructions on the "How to Access Your Online Resources" page found at the front of this book.

In addition to the calculator, you will see instructions for how to use the calculator. Be sure to read these instructions and work through the associated exercises. Throughout our math books, you will see the ⌨ symbol. This symbol means "Use the calculator here!" As much as possible, have the online practice calculator up and running during your review of our math books. You'll have the chance to use the on-screen calculator when you take our practice exams as well.

Navigating the Questions in a Section

Another change for test-takers on the revised GRE is the ability to move freely around the questions in a section—you can go forward and backward one-by-one and can even jump directly to any question from the "review list." The review list provides a snapshot of which questions you have answered, which ones you have tagged for "mark and review," and which are incomplete, either because you didn't indicate enough answers or because you indicated too many (that is, if a number of choices is specified by the question). You should double-check the review list for completion if you finish the section early. Using the review list feature will take some practice as well, which is why we've built it into our online practice exams.

1

The majority of test-takers will be pressed for time. Thus, for some, it won't be feasible to go back to multiple problems at the end of the section. Generally, if you can't get a question the first time, you won't be able to get it the second time around either. With this in mind, here's the order in which we recommend using the new review list feature.

1. Do the questions in the order in which they appear.

2. When you encounter a difficult question, do your best to eliminate answer choices you know are wrong.

3. If you're not sure of an answer, take an educated guess from the choices remaining. Do NOT skip it and hope to return to it later.

4. Using the "mark" button at the top of the screen, mark up to three questions per section that you think you might be able to solve with more time. Mark a question only after you have taken an educated guess.

5. Always click on the review list at the end of a section, to quickly make sure you have neither skipped nor incompletely answered any questions.

6. If you have time, identify any questions that you marked for review and return to them. If you do not have any time remaining, you will have already taken good guesses at the tough ones.

What you want to avoid is surfing—clicking forward and backward through the questions searching for the easy ones. This will eat up valuable time. Of course, you'll want to move through the tough ones quickly if you can't get them, but try to avoid skipping around.

Again, all of this will take practice. Use our practice exams to fine-tune your approach.

Scoring

You need to know two things about the scoring of the revised GRE Verbal Reasoning and Quantitative Reasoning sections: (1) how individual questions influence the score, and (2) the score scale itself.

For both the Verbal Reasoning and Quantitative Reasoning sections, you will receive a scaled score, based on both how many questions you answered correctly and the difficulties of the specific questions you actually saw.

The old GRE was question-adaptive, meaning that your answer to each question (right or wrong) determined, at least somewhat, the questions that followed (harder or easier). Because you had to commit to an answer to let the algorithm do its thing, you weren't allowed to skip questions or to go back to change answers. On the revised GRE, the adapting occurs from section to section rather than from question to question (e.g., if you do well on the first Verbal section, you will get a harder second Verbal section). The only change test-takers will notice is one that most will welcome: you can now move freely about the questions in a section, coming back to tough questions later, changing answers after "Aha!" moments, and generally managing your time more flexibly.

MANHATTAN
PREP

The scores for the revised GRE Quantitative Reasoning and Verbal Reasoning are reported on a 130–170 scale in 1-point increments, whereas the old score reporting was on a 200–800 scale in 10-point increments. You will receive one 130–170 score for Verbal and a separate 130–170 score for Quant. If you are already putting your GRE math skills to work, you may notice that there are now 41 scores possible (170 – 130, then add 1 before you're done), whereas before there were 61 scores possible ([800 – 200]/10, then add 1 before you're done). In other words, a 10-point difference on the old score scale actually indicated a smaller performance differential than a 1-point difference on the new scale. However, the GRE folks argue that perception is reality: the difference between 520 and 530 on the old scale could simply seem greater than the difference between 151 and 152 on the new scale. If that's true, then this change will benefit test-takers, who won't be unfairly compared by schools for minor differences in performance. If not true, then the change is moot.

Question Formats in Detail

Essay Questions

The Analytical Writing section consists of two separately timed 30-minute tasks: Analyze an Issue and Analyze an Argument. As you can imagine, the 30-minute time limit implies that you aren't aiming to write an essay that would garner a Pulitzer Prize nomination, but rather to complete the tasks adequately and according to the directions. Each essay is scored separately, but your reported essay score is the average of the two, rounded up to the next half-point increment on a 0–6 scale.

Issue Task: This essay prompt will present a claim, generally one that is vague enough to be interpreted in various ways and discussed from numerous perspectives. Your job as a test-taker is to write a response discussing the extent to which you agree or disagree and support your position. Don't sit on the fence—pick a side!

For some examples of Issue Task prompts, visit the GRE website here:

> www.ets.org/gre/revised_general/prepare/analytical_writing/issue/pool

Argument Task: This essay prompt will be an argument comprised of both a claim (or claims) and evidence. Your job is to dispassionately discuss the argument's structural flaws and merits (well, mostly the flaws). Don't agree or disagree with the argument—simply evaluate its logic.

For some examples of Argument Task prompts, visit the GRE website here:

> www.ets.org/gre/revised_general/prepare/analytical_writing/argument/pool

1

Verbal: Reading Comprehension Questions

Standard five-choice multiple-choice Reading Comprehension questions continue to appear on the revised exam. You are likely familiar with how these work. Let's take a look at two *new* Reading Comprehension formats that will appear on the revised test.

Select One or More Answer Choices and Select-in-Passage

For the question type "Select One or More Answer Choices," you are given three statements about a passage and asked to "indicate all that apply." Either one, two, or all three can be correct (there is no "none of the above" option). There is no partial credit; you must indicate all of the correct choices and none of the incorrect choices.

Strategy Tip: On "Select One or More Answer Choices," don't let your brain be tricked into telling you, "Well, if two of them have been right so far, the other one must be wrong," or any other arbitrary idea about how many of the choices *should* be correct. Make sure to consider each choice independently! You cannot use "process of elimination" in the same way as you do on normal multiple-choice questions.

For the question type "Select-in-Passage," you are given an assignment such as "Select the sentence in the passage that explains why the experiment's results were discovered to be invalid." Clicking anywhere on the sentence in the passage will highlight it. (As with any GRE question, you will have to click "Confirm" to submit your answer, so don't worry about accidentally selecting the wrong sentence due to a slip of the mouse.)

Strategy Tip: On "Select-in-Passage," if the passage is short, consider numbering each sentence (i.e., writing 1 2 3 4 on your paper) and crossing off each choice as you determine that it isn't the answer. If the passage is long, you might write a number for each paragraph (I, II, III), and tick off each number as you determine that the correct sentence is not located in that paragraph.

Now give these new question types a try:

The sample questions below are based on this passage:

> Physicist Robert Oppenheimer, director of the fateful Manhattan Project, said, "It is a profound and necessary truth that the deep things in science are not found because they are useful; they are found because it was possible to find them." In a later address at MIT, Oppenheimer presented the thesis that scientists could be held only very nominally responsible for the consequences of their research and discovery. Oppenheimer asserted that ethics, philosophy, and politics have very little to do with the day-to-day work of the scientist, and that scientists could not rationally be expected to predict all the effects of their work. Yet, in a talk in 1945 to the Association of Los Alamos Scientists, Oppenheimer offered some reasons why the Manhattan Project scientists built the atomic bomb; the justifications included "fear that Nazi Germany would build it first" and "hope that it would shorten the war."

MANHATTAN
PREP

For question #1, consider each of the three choices separately and indicate all that apply.

1. The passage implies that Robert Oppenheimer would most likely have agreed with which of the following views:

    [A] Some scientists take military goals into account in their work
    [B] Deep things in science are not useful
    [C] The everyday work of a scientist is only minimally involved with ethics

2. Select the sentence in which the writer implies that Oppenheimer has not been consistent in his view that scientists have little consideration for the effects of their work.

(Here, you would highlight the appropriate sentence with your mouse. Note that there are only four options.)

Solutions
=========

1. **(A)** and **(C)**: Oppenheimer says in the last sentence that one of the reasons the bomb was built was scientists' *hope that it would shorten the war.* Thus, Oppenheimer would likely agree with the view that *Some scientists take military goals into account in their work*. (B) is a trap answer using familiar language from the passage. Oppenheimer says that scientific discoveries' possible usefulness is not why scientists make discoveries; he does not say that the discoveries aren't useful. Oppenheimer specifically says that ethics has *very little to do with the day-to-day work of the scientist,* which is a good match for *only minimally involved with ethics.*

Strategy Tip: On "Select One or More Answer Choices," write A B C on your paper and mark each choice with a check, an *X*, or a symbol such as ~ if you're not sure. This should keep you from crossing out all three choices and having to go back (at least one of the choices must be correct). For example, say that on a *different* question you had marked

    A. *X*
    B. ~
    C. *X*

The answer choice you weren't sure about, (B), is likely to be correct, since there must be at least one correct answer.

---

2. The correct sentence is: **Yet, in a talk in 1945 to the Association of Los Alamos Scientists, Oppenheimer offered some reasons why the Manhattan Project scientists built the atomic bomb; the justifications included "fear that Nazi Germany would build it first" and "hope that it would shorten the war."** The word "yet" is a good clue that this sentence is about to express a view contrary to the views expressed in the rest of the passage.

1

Verbal: Text Completion Questions

Text Completions can consist of 1–5 sentences with 1–3 blanks. When Text Completions have two or three blanks, you will select words or short phrases for those blanks independently. There is no partial credit; you must make every selection correctly.

Leaders are not always expected to (i) _____ the same rules as are those they lead; leaders are often looked up to for a surety and presumption that would be viewed as (ii) _____ in most others.

Blank (i)	Blank (ii)
decree	hubris
proscribe	avarice
conform to	anachronism

Select your two choices by actually clicking and highlighting the words you want.

<u>Solution</u>

In the first blank, you need a word similar to "follow." In the second blank, you need a word similar to "arrogance." The correct answers are *conform to* and *hubris*.

Strategy Tip: Do NOT look at the answer choices until you've decided for yourself, based on textual clues actually written in the sentence, what kind of word needs to go in each blank. Only then should you look at the choices and eliminate those that are not matches.

Now try an example with three blanks:

For Kant, the fact of having a right and having the (i) _____ to enforce it via coercion cannot be separated, and he asserts that this marriage of rights and coercion is compatible with the freedom of everyone. This is not at all peculiar from the standpoint of modern political thought—what good is a right if its violation triggers no enforcement (be it punishment or (ii) _____)? The necessity of coercion is not at all in conflict with the freedom of everyone, because this coercion only comes into play when someone has (iii) _____ someone else.

Blank (i)	Blank (ii)	Blank (iii)
technique	amortization	questioned the hypothesis of
license	reward	violated the rights of
prohibition	restitution	granted civil liberties to

Solution

In the first sentence, use the clue "he asserts that this marriage of rights and coercion is compatible with the freedom of everyone" to help fill in the first blank. Kant believes that "coercion" is "married to" rights and is compatible with freedom for all. So you want something in the first blank like "right" or "power." Kant believes that rights are meaningless without enforcement. Only the choice *license* can work (while a *license* can be physical, like a driver's license, *license* can also mean "right").

The second blank is part of the phrase "punishment or _____," which you are told is the "enforcement" resulting from the violation of a right. So the blank should be something, other than punishment, that constitutes enforcement against someone who violates a right. (More simply, it should be something bad.) Only *restitution* works. Restitution is compensating the victim in some way (perhaps monetarily or by returning stolen goods).

In the final sentence, "coercion only comes into play when someone has _____ someone else." Throughout the text, "coercion" means enforcement against someone who has violated the rights of someone else. The meaning is the same here. The answer is *violated the rights of*.

The complete and correct answer is this combination:

Blank (i)	Blank (ii)	Blank (iii)
license	restitution	violated the rights of

In theory, there are 3 × 3 × 3, or 27 possible ways to answer a three-blank Text Completion—and only one of those 27 ways is correct. In theory, these are bad odds. In practice, you will often have certainty about some of the blanks, so your guessing odds are almost never this bad. Just follow the basic process: come up with your own filler for each blank, and match to the answer choices. If you're confused by this example, don't worry! The Manhattan Prep *Text Completion & Sentence Equivalence GRE Strategy Guide* covers all of this in detail.

Strategy Tip: Do not write your own story. The GRE cannot give you a blank without also giving you a clue, physically written down in the passage, telling you what kind of word or phrase must go in that blank. Find that clue. You should be able to give textual evidence for each answer choice you select.

Verbal: Sentence Equivalence Questions

For this question type, you are given one sentence with a single blank. There are six answer choices, and you are asked to pick two choices that fit the blank and are alike in meaning.

Of the Verbal question types, this one depends the most on vocabulary and also yields the most to strategy.

1

No partial credit is given on Sentence Equivalence; both correct answers must be selected and no incorrect answers may be selected. When you pick 2 of 6 choices, there are 15 possible combinations of choices, and only one is correct. However, this is not nearly as daunting as it sounds.

Think of it this way: if you have six choices, but the two correct ones must be similar in meaning, then you have, at most, three possible *pairs* of choices, maybe fewer, since not all choices are guaranteed to have a partner. If you can match up the pairs, you can seriously narrow down your options.

Here is a sample set of answer choices:

- [A] tractable
- [B] taciturn
- [C] arbitrary
- [D] tantamount
- [E] reticent
- [F] amenable

The question is deliberately omitted here in order to illustrate how much you can do with the choices alone, if you have studied vocabulary sufficiently.

Tractable and *amenable* are synonyms (tractable, amenable people will do whatever you want them to do). *Taciturn* and *reticent* are synonyms (both mean "not talkative").

Arbitrary (based on one's own will) and *tantamount* (equivalent) are not similar in meaning and therefore cannot be a pair. Therefore, the *only* possible correct answer pairs are (A) and (F), and (B) and (E). You have improved your chances from 1 in 15 to a 50/50 shot without even reading the question!

Of course, in approaching a Sentence Equivalence, you do want to analyze the sentence in the same way you would a Text Completion—read for a textual clue that tells you what type of word *must* go in the blank. Then look for a matching pair.

Strategy Tip: If you're sure that a word in the choices does *not* have a partner, cross it out! For instance, if (A) and (F) are partners and (B) and (E) are partners, and you're sure neither (C) nor (D) pair with any other answer, cross out (C) and (D) completely. They cannot be the answer together, nor can either one be part of the answer.

The sentence for the answer choice above could read as follows:

> Though the dinner guests were quite _____ , the hostess did her best to keep the conversation active and engaging.

Thus, **(B)** and **(E)** are the best choices.

Try another example:

While athletes usually expect to achieve their greatest feats in their teens or twenties, opera singers don't reach the _____ of their vocal powers until middle age.

    [A]   harmony
    [B]   zenith
    [C]   acme
    [D]   terminus
    [E]   nadir
    [F]   cessation

Solution

Those with strong vocabularies might go straight to the choices to make pairs. *Zenith* and *acme* are synonyms, meaning "high point, peak." *Terminus* and *cessation* are synonyms meaning "end." *Nadir* is a low point and *harmony* is present here as a trap answer reminding you of opera singers. Cross off (A) and (E), since they do not have partners. Then, go back to the sentence, knowing that your only options are a pair meaning "peak" and a pair meaning "end."

The correct answer choices are **(B)** and **(C)**.

Math: Quantitative Comparison

In addition to regular multiple-choice questions and Data Interpretation questions, Quantitative Comparisons have been on the exam for a long time.

Each question contains a "Quantity A" and a "Quantity B," and some also contain common information that applies to both quantities. The four answer choices are always worded exactly as shown in the following example:

$$x \geq 0$$

Quantity A	**Quantity B**
x	x^2

(A)   Quantity A is greater.

(B)   Quantity B is greater.

(C)   The two quantities are equal.

(D)   The relationship cannot be determined from the information given.

1

Solution

If $x = 0$, then the two quantities are equal. If $x = 2$, then Quantity (B) is greater. Thus, you don't have enough information.

The answer is **(D)**.

Next, take a look at the new math question formats.

Math: Select One or More Answer Choices

According to the *Official Guide to the GRE revised General Test*, the official directions for "Select One or More Answer Choices" read as follows:

> Directions: Select one or more answer choices according to the specific question directions.
>
> If the question does not specify how many answer choices to indicate, indicate all that apply.
>
> The correct answer may be just one of the choices or as many as all of the choices, depending on the question.
>
> No credit is given unless you indicate all of the correct choices and no others.
>
> If the question specifies how many answer choices to indicate, indicate exactly that number of choices.

Note that there is no partial credit. If three of six choices are correct, and you indicate two of the three, no credit is given. If you are told to indicate two choices and you indicate three, no credit is given. It will also be important to read the directions carefully.

Here's a sample question:

If $ab = |a| \times |b|$ and $ab \neq 0$, which of the following must be true?

Indicate <u>all</u> such statements.

A $a = b$
B $a > 0$ and $b > 0$
C $ab > 0$

Note that only one, only two, or all three of the choices may be correct. (Also note the word "must" in the question stem!)

MANHATTAN
PREP

Solution

If $ab = |a| \times |b|$, then you know ab is positive, since the right side of the equation must be positive. If ab is positive, however, that doesn't necessarily mean that a and b are each positive; it simply means that they have the same sign.

Answer choice (A) is not correct because it is not true that a must equal b; for instance, a could be 2 and b could be 3.

Answer choice (B) is not correct because it is not true that a and b must each be positive; for instance, a could be −3 and b could be −4.

Now look at choice (C). Since $|a| \times |b|$ must be positive, ab must be positive as well; that is, since two sides of an equation are, by definition, equal to one another, if one side of the equation is positive, the other side must be positive as well. Thus, answer **(C)** is correct.

Strategy Tip: Make sure to fully process the statement in the question (simplify it or list the possible scenarios) before considering the answer choices. That is, don't just look at $ab = |a| \times |b|$—rather, it's your job to draw inferences about the statement before plowing ahead. This will save you time in the long run!

Note that "indicate all that apply" didn't really make the problem harder. This is just a typical Inference-based Quant problem (for more problems like this one, see the Manhattan Prep *Number Properties* guide as well as the *Quantitative Comparisons & Data Interpretation* guide).

After all, not every real-life problem has exactly five possible solutions; why should problems on the GRE?

Math: Numeric Entry

This question type requires the test-taker to key a numeric answer into a box on the screen. You are not able to work backwards from answer choices, and in many cases, it will be difficult to make a guess. However, the principles being tested are the same as on the rest of the exam.

Here is a sample question:

If $x \triangle y = 2xy - (x - y)$, what is the value of $3 \triangle 4$?

Solution

You are given a function involving two variables, *x* and *y*, and asked to substitute 3 for *x* and 4 for *y*:

$$x\Delta y = 2xy - (x - y)$$
$$3\Delta 4 = 2(3)(4) - (3 - 4)$$
$$3\Delta 4 = 24 - (-1)$$
$$3\Delta 4 = 25$$

The answer is **25**.

Thus, you would type 25 into the box.

Okay. You've now got a good start on understanding the structure and question formats of the new GRE. Now it's time to begin fine-tuning your skills.

MANHATTAN
PREP

Chapter 2

of

Geometry

Geometry Problem Solving

In This Chapter...

Using Equations to Solve Geometry Problems

Chapter 2
Geometry Problem Solving

Using Equations to Solve Geometry Problems

Before you dive into the specific properties of the many shapes tested on the GRE, it's important to establish a foundation of translating the information presented in questions into algebraic equations. This will allow you to more easily, and quickly, solve even the most complex geometry problems. To start, try the following problem:

Rectangles *ABCD* and *EFGH*, shown below, have equal areas. The length of side *AB* is 5. What is the length of diagonal *AC*?

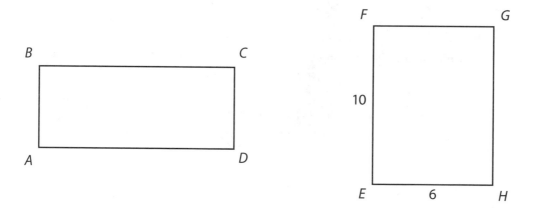

The first step in any geometry question involving shapes is to draw your own copies of the shapes on your note paper and fill in everything you know. In this problem in particular, you would want to redraw both rectangles and add to your picture the information that side *AB* has a length of 5. Also, make note of what you're looking for—in this case you want the length of diagonal *AC*. So your new figures would look like this:

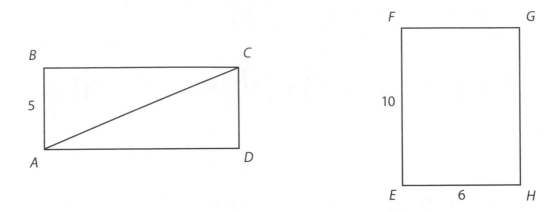

Now that you have redrawn your figures and filled in all the given information, it's time to begin answering the question.

So the question now becomes, has the problem provided you any information that can be expressed mathematically? In other words, can you create equations? Well, it did tell you one thing that you can use—the two rectangles have equal areas. So you can say that Area$_{ABCD}$ = Area$_{EFGH}$. But you can do better than that. The formula for the area of a rectangle is Area = (length) × (width). So your equation can be rewritten as (length$_{ABCD}$) × (width$_{ABCD}$) = (length$_{EFGH}$) × (width$_{EFGH}$).

The length and width of rectangle *EFGH* are 6 and 10 (it doesn't matter which is which), and the length of *AB* is 5. So your equation becomes (5) × (width$_{ABCD}$) = (6) × (10). So (5) × (width$_{ABCD}$) = 60, which means that the width of rectangle *ABCD* is 60/5, which equals 12.

Any time you learn a new piece of information (in this case the width of rectangle *ABCD*), you should put that information into your picture. So your picture of rectangle *ABCD* now looks like this:

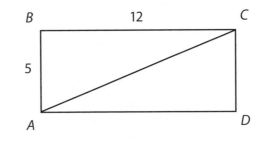

To recap what you've done so far, you started this problem by redrawing the shapes described in the question and filling in all the information (such as side lengths, angles, etc.) that you knew, and made note of the value the question was asking you for. The first step for geometry problems is to **draw or redraw figures and fill in all given information**. Of course, you should also confirm what you're being asked!

MANHATTAN
PREP

Next, you made use of additional information provided in the question. The question stated that the two rectangles had equal areas. You created an equation to express this relationship, and then plugged in the values you knew (length and width of rectangle *EFGH* and length of rectangle *ABCD*), and solved for the width of rectangle *ABCD*. You **identified relationships and created equations**. After that, you **solved the equations for the missing value** (in this case, the width of rectangle *ABCD*).

In some ways, all you have done so far is set up the problem. In fact, aside from noting that you need to find the length of diagonal *AC*, nothing you have done so far seems to have directly helped you actually solve for that value. The work you've done to this point let you find that the width of rectangle *ABCD* is 12.

So why did you bother solving for the width of rectangle *ABCD* when you didn't even know why you would need it? The answer is that there is a very good chance that you will need that value in order to answer the question.

There was no way initially to find the length of diagonal *AC*. You simply did not have enough information. The question did, however, provide you enough information to find the width of rectangle *ABCD*. More often than not, if you have enough information to solve for a value, you need that value to answer the question.

So the question now becomes, what can you do now that you know the width of rectangle *ABCD* that you couldn't do before? To answer that, take another look at the value you're looking for: the length of *AC*.

As mentioned earlier, an important part of problem solving is to identify relationships. You already identified the relationship mentioned in the question—that both rectangles have equal areas. But, for many geometry problems, there are additional relationships that aren't as obvious.

The key to this problem is to recognize that *AC* is not only the diagonal of rectangle *ABCD*, but is also the hypotenuse of a right triangle. You know this because one property of rectangles is that all four interior angles are right angles:

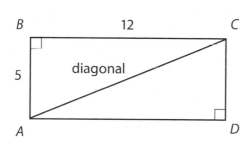

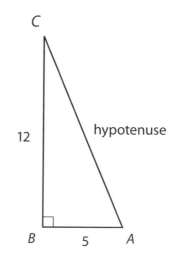

Now that you know AC is the hypotenuse of a right triangle, you can use the Pythagorean theorem to find the length of the hypotenuse using the two side lengths.

Sides BC and BA are the legs of the triangle, and AC is the hypotenuse, so:

$$(BC)^2 + (BA)^2 = (AC)^2$$
$$(12)^2 + (5)^2 = (AC)^2$$
$$144 + 25 = (AC)^2$$
$$169 = (AC)^2$$
$$13 = AC$$

Alternatively, you can avoid that work by recognizing that this triangle is one of the Pythagorean triples: a 5–12–13 triangle. Either way, the answer to the question is diagonal AC equals 13.

Now recap what occurred in the last portion of this question. The process that allowed you to solve for the width of rectangle $ABCD$ was based on information explicitly presented to you in the question. To proceed from there, however, required a different sort of process. The key insight was that the diagonal of rectangle $ABCD$ was also the hypotenuse of right triangle ABC. Additionally, you needed to know that, in order to find the length of AC, you needed the lengths of the other two sides of the triangle. The last part of this problem required you to **make inferences from the figures**. Sometimes, these inferences required you to make a jump from one shape to another through a common element. For instance, you needed to see AC as both a diagonal of a rectangle and as a hypotenuse of a right triangle. Here, AC was the common element in both a rectangle and a right triangle. Other times, these inferences will make you think about what information you would need in order to find another value.

Before you go through another sample problem, it's a good idea to revisit the important steps to answering geometry problems.

Recap

Step 1: **Draw or redraw figures and fill in all given information.**
Fill in all known angles and lengths and make note of any equal sides or angles.

Step 2: **Identify relationships and create equations.**
Often, these relationships will be explicitly stated in the question.

Step 3: **Solve the equations for the missing value(s).**
If you can solve for a value, you will often need that value to answer the question.

Step 4: **Make inferences from the figures.**
You will often need to make use of relationships that are not explicitly stated.

Now that you've got the basic process down, try another problem. Try it on your own first, then look at the steps used to solve it:

> Rectangle *PQRS* is inscribed in circle *O* pictured below. If the circumference of circle *O* is 5π, what is the area of rectangle *PQRS*?

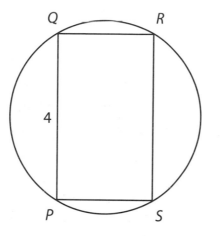

The first thing you need to do is to **redraw the figure** on whatever note paper you are using and **fill in all the given information**. The question didn't explicitly give you the value of any side lengths or angles, but it did say that *PQRS* is a rectangle. That means all four internal angles are right angles. So when you redraw the figure, it might look like this:

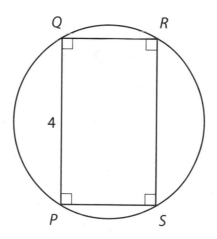

Now it's time to **identify relationships and create equations**. The question stated that the circumference of circle *O* is 5π, and the formula for circumference is circumference equals $2\pi r$, so $5\pi = 2\pi r$. Now that you know the circumference, there's only one unknown (r), so you should **solve the equation for the missing value** and find the radius, which turns out to be 2.5. You also know that $d = 2r$, so the diameter of circle *O* is 5.

As with the previous problem, you are now left with the question: Why did you find the radius and diameter? You were able to solve for them, which is a very good clue that you need one of them to answer the question. Now is the time to **make inferences from the figures**.

Ultimately, this question is asking for the area of rectangle *PQRS*. What information do you need to find that value? You have the length of *QP*, which means that if you can find the length of either *QR* or *PS*, you can find the area of the rectangle. So you need to somehow find a connection between the rectangle and the radius or diameter. Put a diameter into the circle:

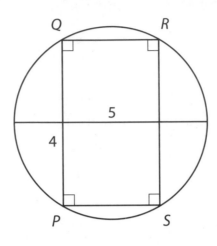

That didn't really seem to help much, because you still have no way to make the connection between the diameter and the rectangle. It's important to remember, though, that *any* line that passes through the center is a diameter. What if you drew the diameter so that it passed through the center but touched the circle at points *P* and *R*? You know that the line connecting points *P* and *R* will be a diameter because you know that the center of the circle is also the center of the rectangle. Your circle now looks like this:

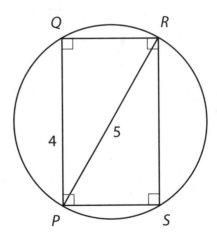

What was the advantage of drawing the diameter so that it connected points *P* and *R*? Now the diameter of the circle is also the diagonal of the rectangle. The circle and the rectangle have a common element. **Whenever possible, draw new elements such that they relate one shape to another.**

MANHATTAN
PREP

Where do you go from here? You still need the length of either *QR* or *PS*. Do you have a way to get either one of those values? As a matter of fact, you do. *PQR* is a right triangle. It's not oriented the way you are used to seeing it, but all the important elements are there. It's a triangle, and one of its internal angles is a right angle. Additionally, you know the lengths of two of the sides: *PQ* and *PR*. That means you can use the Pythagorean theorem to find the length of the third side, *QR*:

$$(QR)^2 + (PQ)^2 = (PR)^2$$
$$(QR)^2 + (4)^2 = (5)^2$$
$$(QR)^2 + 16 = 25$$
$$(QR)^2 = 9$$
$$QR = 3$$

Alternatively, you could have recognized the Pythagorean triple: triangle *PQR* is a 3–4–5 triangle. Either way, you arrive at the conclusion that the length of *QR* is 3. Your circle now looks like this:

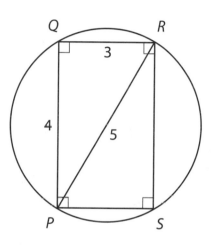

Now you have what you need to find the area of rectangle *PQRS*: Area = (length) × (width) = (4) × (3) = 12. So the answer to the question is 12.

What did you need to do in order to arrive at that answer? For starters, you needed to make sure that you had an accurate figure to work with, and that you populated that figure with all the information that you had been given. Next, you had to realize that knowing the circumference of the circle allowed you to find the diameter of the circle.

After that came what is often the most difficult part of the process—you had to make inferences based on the figure. The key insight in this problem was that you could draw a diameter in your figure that could also act as the diagonal of the rectangle. As if that wasn't difficult enough, you then had to recognize that *PQR* was a right triangle, even though it was rotated in a way that made this difficult to see. It is these kinds of insights that are going to be crucial to success on the GRE—recognizing shapes when they're presented in an unfamiliar format and finding connections between different shapes.

2

<u>Check Your Skills</u>

1. In rectangle *ABCD*, the distance between *B* and *D* is 10. What is the area of the circle inside the rectangle, if the circle is tangent to both *AD* and *BC*?

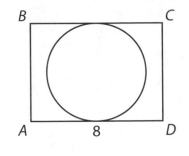

The answer can be found on page 39.

Check Your Skills Answer Key

2

1. **9π:** Consider only the rectangle for a moment. Diagonal *BD* cuts the rectangle into two right triangles, and the length of this diagonal is given:

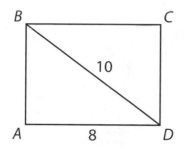

Now look at right triangle *ABD*. The line segment *BD* functions not only as the diagonal of rectangle *ABCD* but also as the hypotenuse of right triangle *ABD*. So now find the third side of triangle *ABD*, either using the Pythagorean theorem or recognizing a Pythagorean triple (6–8–10):

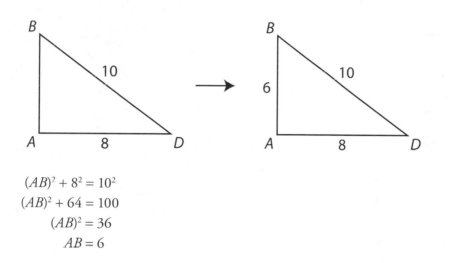

$$(AB)^2 + 8^2 = 10^2$$
$$(AB)^2 + 64 = 100$$
$$(AB)^2 = 36$$
$$AB = 6$$

Now consider the circle within this 6 by 8 rectangle:

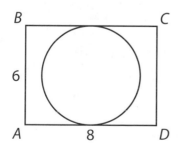

Since the circle touches both *AD* and *BC*, its diameter must be 6.

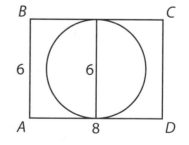

Finally, find the radius and compute the area:

$d = 6 = 2r$ Area $= \pi r^2$

$3 = r$ Area $= \pi 3^2$

                      Area $= 9\pi$

Problem Set

1. The "aspect ratio" of a rectangular TV screen is the ratio of its width to its height.

Quantity A

The area of a rectangular TV screen with an aspect ratio of 4 : 3 and a diagonal of 25"

Quantity B

The area of a rectangular TV screen with an aspect ratio of 16 : 9 and a diagonal of 25"

2. Ten 8-foot-long poles will be arranged in a rectangle to surround a flower bed.

Quantity A

The area in square feet of the flower bed

Quantity B

300

3.

BCDF and ABDE are squares.

Quantity A

Twice the area of the shaded region

Quantity B

Three times the area of BCDF

Solutions

1. **(A):** For the TV in Quantity A, the aspect ratio of 4 : 3 means the width is $4x$ and the height is $3x$, where x is some unknown multiplier. By Pythagorean theorem, the diagonal is: $\sqrt{a^2+b^2} = \sqrt{(4x)^2+(3x)^2} = \sqrt{16x^2+9x^2} - \sqrt{25x^2} = 5x$. You know that the diagonal is 25 inches, so x is 5. The width of the TV is (4)(5), which is 20, and the height is (3)(5), which is 15. Thus, the area is $wh = (20)(15)$, which equals 300.

For the TV in Quantity B, the aspect ratio of 16 : 9 means the width is $16y$ and the height is $9y$, where y is some unknown multiplier. By Pythagorean theorem, the diagonal is: $\sqrt{a^2+b^2} = \sqrt{(16y)^2+(9y)^2} = \sqrt{256y^2+81y^2} = \sqrt{337y^2} \approx 18.3576y$ (use the calculator!). You know that the diagonal is 25 inches, so $y \approx \dfrac{25}{18.3576} \approx 1.3618$. The width of the TV is approximately (16)(1.3618), which is 21.7888, and the height is approximately (9)(1.3618), which is 12.2562. Thus, the area is (width)(height) = (21.7888)(12.2562), which equals 267.05.

Thus, **Quantity A is greater**.

Incidentally, you will learn a shortcut for this problem in Chapter 4 of this guide (in the section "Maximum Area of Polygons"). For a TV with a fixed perimeter (or here the diagonal, which similarly depends on the width and height), the area is maximized when the aspect ratio is 1. Since the aspect ratio 4 : 3 (equivalent to $\dfrac{4}{3} = 1.\overline{3}$) is closer to 1 than the aspect ratio 16 : 9 (equivalent to $\dfrac{16}{9} = 1.\overline{7}$), the TV with the 4 : 3 aspect ratio has a greater area.

2. **(D):** First, **draw the figure and fill in all given information**. The flower bed might look like this:

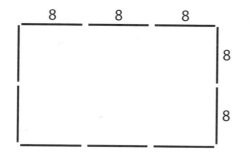

Or like this:

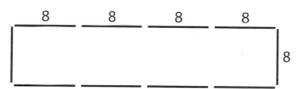

Then, **make inferences from the figures**. The area of a rectangle equals the width times the height. The top flower bed has an area of $(2 \times 8)(3 \times 8) = (16)(24) = 384$, which is greater than 300. The bottom flower bed has an area of $(1 \times 8)(4 \times 8) = (8)(32) = 256$, which is less than 300.

Therefore, **the relationship cannot be determined from the information given**.

3. **(C):** Since no lengths are given, you are free to pick some easy numbers to work with. **Draw the figure and fill in all given information**, which here is that the figures are squares. For the sides of the small square, 1 is an easy number, as it makes the area of square *BCDF* equal (1)(1), which is 1:

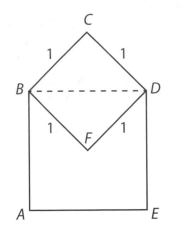

Next, identify relationships. The figure implies that the dashed line *BD* is both an edge of square *ABDE* and the diagonal of square *BCDF*, making it the hypotenuse of equal right triangles *BCD* and *BDF*. By Pythagorean theorem on right triangle *BCD*, you get the following:

$$c^2 = a^2 + b^2$$
$$BD^2 = 1^2 + 1^2$$
$$BD^2 = 2$$
$$BD = \sqrt{2}$$

Thus, the area of square *ABDE* is $\sqrt{2} \times \sqrt{2} = 2$.

Make inferences from the figure: The shaded area is the area of square *ABDE* minus half the area of square *BCDF*. The shaded area is $2 - \dfrac{1}{2} = \dfrac{3}{2}$.

Quantity A is 2 times the shaded area, or $2 \times \dfrac{3}{2} = 3$.

Quantity B is 3 times the area of *BCDF*, or $3 \times 1 = 3$.

Thus, **the two quantities are equal**.

Chapter 3 of Geometry

Triangles & Diagonals

In This Chapter...

Chapter 3
Triangles & Diagonals

The Basic Properties of a Triangle

Triangles show up all over the GRE. You'll often find them hiding in problems that seem to be about rectangles or other shapes. Of the basic shapes, triangles are perhaps the most challenging to master. One reason is that several properties of triangles are tested.

Following are some general comments on triangles.

The sum of any two side lengths of a triangle will always be greater than the third side length. This is because the shortest distance between two points is a straight line. At the same time, the third side length will always be greater than the difference of the other two side lengths. The pictures below illustrate these two points:

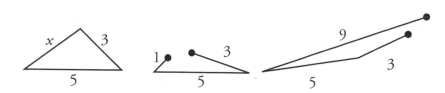

What is the largest number x could be? What's the smallest? Observe what happens when you try to make $x = 9$ or $x = 1$:

> x must be less than $3 + 5 = 8$
> x must be greater than $5 - 3 = 2$
> $2 < x < 8$

Check Your Skills

1. Two sides of a triangle have lengths of 5 and 19. Can the third side have a length of 13?
2. Two sides of a triangle have lengths of 8 and 17. What is the range of possible values of the length of the third side?

Answers can be found on page 61.

The internal angles of a triangle must add up to 180°. This rule can sometimes allow you to make inferences about angles of unknown size. It means that if you know the measures of two angles in the triangle, you can determine the measure of the third angle. Take a look at this triangle:

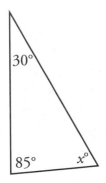

The three internal angles must add up to 180°, so you know that $30 + 85 + x = 180$. Solving for x tells you that $x = 65$, so the third angle is 65°. The GRE can also test your knowledge of this rule in more complicated ways. Take a look at this triangle:

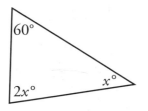

In this situation, you only know one of the angles. The other two are given in terms of x. Even though you only know one angle, you can still determine the other two. Again, you know that the three angles will add up to 180°, so $60 + x + 2x = 180$. That means that $3x = 120$, so $x = 40$. Thus, the angle labeled $x°$ has a measure of 40° and the angle labeled $2x°$ has a measure of 80°.

The GRE will not always draw triangles to scale, so don't try to guess angles from the picture, which could be distorted. Instead, solve for angles mathematically.

Check Your Skills

Find the missing angle(s).

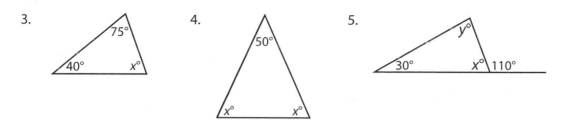

3.
4.
5.

Answers can be found on page 61.

Internal angles of a triangle are important on the GRE for another reason. **Sides correspond to their opposite angles.** This means that **the longest side is opposite the largest angle, and the smallest side is opposite the smallest angle**. Think about an alligator opening its mouth, bigger and bigger… as the angle between its upper and lower jaws increases, the distance between the front teeth on the bottom and top would get longer and longer. This is illustrated below:

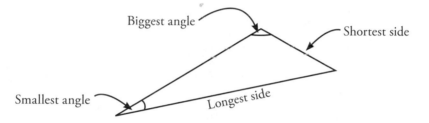

One important thing to remember about this relationship is that it works both ways. If you know the sides of the triangle, you can make inferences about the angles. If you know the angles, you can make inferences about the sides, as shown below.

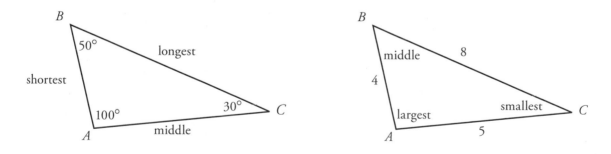

Although you can determine from the angle measures which sides are longer or shorter, you cannot determine how *much* longer or shorter. For instance, in the triangle on the left above, $\angle BAC$ is twice as large as $\angle ABC$, but that does *not* mean that BC is twice as long as AC.

Things get interesting when a triangle has sides that are the same length or angles that have the same measure. You can classify triangles by the number of equal sides that they have:

- A triangle that has two equal angles and two equal sides (opposite the equal angles) is an **isosceles triangle**.

- A triangle that has three equal angles (all 60°) and three equal sides is an **equilateral triangle**.

Once again, it is important to remember that this relationship between equal angles and equal sides works in both directions. Take a look at these isosceles triangles, and think about what additional information you can infer from them:

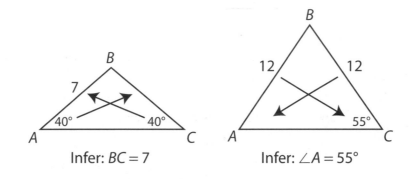

The GRE loves isosceles triangles and uses them in a variety of ways. The following is a more challenging application of the equal sides/equal angles rule:

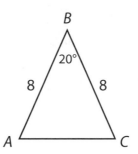

Take a look at the triangle and see what other information you can fill in. Specifically, do you know the degree measure of either ∠*BAC* or ∠*ACB*?

Because side *AB* is the same length as side *BC*, you know that ∠*BAC* has the same degree measure as ∠*ACB*. For convenience, you could label each of those angles as *x*° on your diagram:

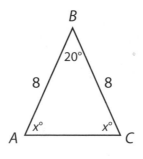

MANHATTAN
PREP

You also know that the three internal angles will add up to 180°, so $20 + x + x = 180$. Thus, $2x = 160$, and $x = 80$. So $\angle BAC$ and $\angle ACB$ each equal 80°. You can't find the side length AC without more advanced math, but the GRE wouldn't ask you for the length of AC for that very reason.

Check Your Skills

Find the value of x.

6.
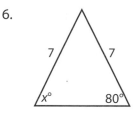

7.
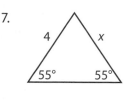

8.
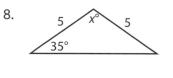

Answers can be found on page 62.

Perimeter and Area

The **perimeter** of a triangle is the sum of the lengths of all three sides.

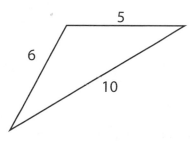

In the triangle above, the perimeter is: $5 + 6 + 10 = 21$. This is a relatively simple property of a triangle, so often it will be used in combination with another property. Try this next problem. What is the perimeter of triangle PQR?

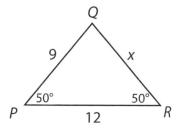

To solve for the perimeter, you will need to determine the value of x. Because angles QPR and PRQ are both 50°, you know that their opposite sides will have equal lengths. That means sides PQ and QR must have equal lengths, so you can infer that side QR has a length of 9. The perimeter of triangle PQR is: $9 + 9 + 12 = 30$.

Check Your Skills

Find the perimeter of each triangle.

9.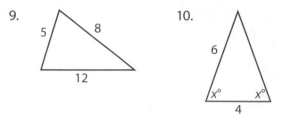

10.

Answers can be found on page 62.

Note: Figures not drawn to scale. You need to be ready to solve geometry problems without depending on exactly accurate figures.

The final property of a triangle to review is area. You may be familiar with the equation

Area = $\frac{1}{2}$ **(base)** × **(height)**.

One very important thing to understand about the area of a triangle (and area in general) is the relationship between the base and the height. The base and the height MUST be perpendicular to each other. In a triangle, one side of the triangle is the base, and the height is formed by dropping a line from the opposite point of the triangle straight down towards the base, so that it forms a 90° angle with the base. The small square located where the height and base meet (shown in the figure below) is a very common symbol used to denote a right angle.

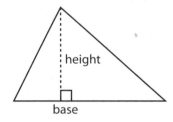

An additional challenge on the GRE is that problems will ask you about familiar shapes but present them to you in orientations you are not accustomed to. Even the area of a triangle can be affected. Most people generally think of the base of the triangle as the bottom side of the triangle, but, in reality, any side of the triangle could act as a base. In fact, depending on the orientation of the triangle, there may not actually be a bottom side. The three triangles below are all the same triangle, but each one has a different side as the base, and the corresponding height is drawn in.

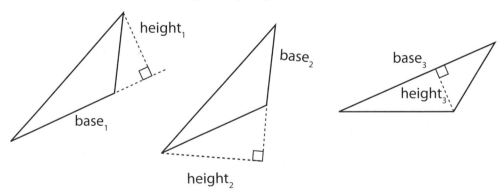

As it turns out, not only can any side be the base, but the height might be drawn outside the triangle! The only thing that matters is that the base and the height are perpendicular to each other.

<u>Check Your Skills</u>

Determine the areas of the following triangles.

11.   12.

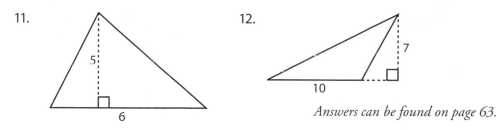

Answers can be found on page 63.

Right Triangles

3

There is one more class of triangle that is very common on the GRE: the **right triangle**. A right triangle is any triangle in which one of the angles is a right angle. The reason such triangles are so important will become more clear as you attempt to answer the next question:

What is the perimeter of triangle *ABC*?

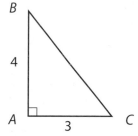

Normally, you would be unable to answer this question. You only have two sides of the triangle, but you need all three sides to calculate the perimeter.

The reason you can answer this question is that right triangles have an additional property that the GRE likes to make use of: there is a consistent relationship among the lengths of its sides. This relationship is known as the **Pythagorean theorem**. For *any* right triangle, the relationship is $a^2 + b^2 = c^2$, where a and b are the lengths of the sides forming the right angle, also known as **legs**, and c is the length of the side opposite the right angle, also known as the **hypotenuse**.

In the triangle above, sides *AB* and *AC* are a and b (it doesn't matter which is which) and side *BC* is c. Thus, $(3)^2 + (4)^2 = (BC)^2 = 9 + 16 = (BC)^2$, so $25 = (BC)^2$, which makes the length of side *BC* equal to 5. The triangle really looks like this:

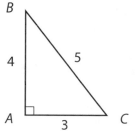

Finally, the perimeter is: $3 + 4 + 5 = 12$.

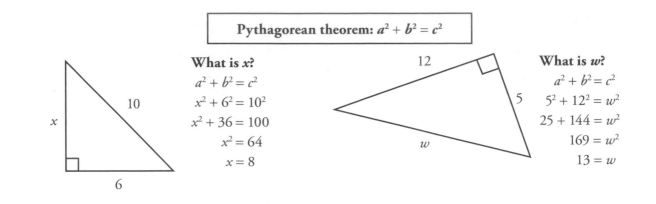

3　Pythagorean Triples

As mentioned above, right triangles show up in many problems on the GRE, and many of these problems require the Pythagorean theorem. But there is a shortcut that you can use in many situations to make the calculations easier.

The GRE favors a certain subset of right triangles in which all three sides have lengths that are integer values. The triangle above was an example of that. The lengths of the sides were 3, 4, and 5—all integers. This group of side lengths is a **Pythagorean triple**—in this case a 3–4–5 triangle. Although there is an infinite number of Pythagorean triples, a few are likely to appear on the test and should be memorized. For each triple, the first two numbers are the lengths of the sides that *form the right angle*, and the third (and largest) number is the *length of the hypotenuse*. They are:

Common Combinations	Key Multiples
3–4–5	6–8–10
The most popular of all right triangles:	9–12–15
$3^2 + 4^2 = 5^2$ (9 + 16 = 25)	12–16–20
5–12–13	
Also quite popular on the GRE:	10–24–26
$5^2 + 12^2 = 13^2$ (25 + 144 = 169)	
8–15–17	
This one appears less frequently:	
$8^2 + 15^2 = 17^2$ (64 + 225 = 289)	None

Warning! Even as you memorize these triangles, don't assume that all triangles fall into these categories. When using common combinations to solve a problem, be sure that the triangle is a right triangle, and that the largest side (hypotenuse) corresponds to the largest number in the triple. For example, if you have a right triangle with one side measuring 3 and the hypotenuse measuring 4, *Do not* conclude that the remaining side is 5.

That being said, try a practice question to see how memorizing these triples can save you time on the GRE:

What is the area of triangle *DEF*?

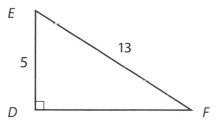

What do you need in order to find the area of triangle *DEF*? The formula for the area of this triangle is area = $\frac{1}{2}$ (base) × (height), so you need a base and a height. This is a right triangle, so sides *DE* and *DF* are perpendicular to each other, which means that if you can figure out the length of side *DF*, you can calculate the area.

The question then becomes, how do you find the length of side *DF*? First, realize that you can *always* find the length of the third side of a right triangle if you know the lengths of the other two sides. That's because you know the Pythagorean theorem. In this case, the formula would look like this: $(DE)^2 + (DF)^2 = (EF)^2$. You know the lengths of two of those sides, so you could rewrite the equation as $(5)^2 + (DF)^2 = (13)^2$. Solving this equation, you get $25 + (DF)^2 = 169$, so $(DF)^2 = 144$, which means *DF* is 12. But these calculations are unnecessary; once you see a right triangle in which one of the legs has a length of 5 and the hypotenuse has a length of 13, you should recognize the Pythagorean triple. The length of the other leg must be 12.

However you find the length of side *DF*, your triangle now looks like this:

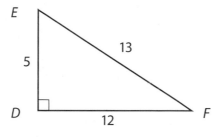

Now you have what you need to find the area of triangle *DEF*: $\frac{1}{2}(12) \times (5) = 6 \times 5 = 30$. Note that in a right triangle, you can consider one leg the base and the other leg the height.

Check Your Skills

For questions 13–14, find the length of the third side of the triangle.

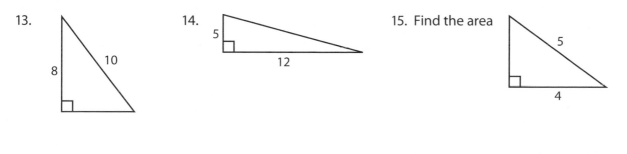

13.   14.   15. Find the area

16. What is the length of hypotenuse *C*? (pictured right)

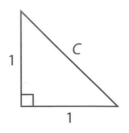

17. What is the length of leg *B*? (pictured right)

18. Triangle *ABC* is isosceles. If *AB* = 3, and *BC* = 4, what are the possible lengths of *AC*?

Answers can be found on page 63.

Isosceles Triangles and the 45–45–90 Triangle

As previously noted, an isosceles triangle is one in which two sides are equal. The two angles opposite those two sides will also be equal. The most important isosceles triangle on the GRE is the isosceles right triangle.

An isosceles right triangle has one 90° angle (opposite the hypotenuse) and two 45° angles (opposite the two equal legs). This triangle is called the 45–45–90 triangle.

The lengths of the legs of every 45–45–90 triangle have a specific ratio, which you must memorize:

$$
\begin{array}{ccccc}
45° & \to & 45° & \to & 90° \\
\text{leg} & & \text{leg} & & \text{hypotenuse} \\
1 & : & 1 & : & \sqrt{2} \\
x & : & x & : & x\sqrt{2}
\end{array}
$$

What does it mean that the sides of a 45–45–90 triangle are in a $1 : 1 : \sqrt{2}$ ratio? It doesn't mean that they are actually 1, 1, and $\sqrt{2}$ (although that's a possibility). It means that the sides are some multiple of $1 : 1 : \sqrt{2}$. For instance, they could be 2, 2, and $2\sqrt{2}$, or 5.5, 5.5, and $5.5\sqrt{2}$. In the last two cases, the number you multiplied the ratio by—either 2 or 5.5—is called the **multiplier**. Using a multiplier of 2

MANHATTAN
PREP

has the same effect as doubling a recipe—each of the ingredients gets doubled. Of course, you can also triple a recipe or multiply it by any other number, even a fraction. Try this problem:

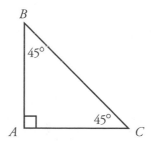

If the length of side *AB* is 5, what are the lengths of sides *BC* and *AC*?

Since *AB* is 5, use the ratio $1 : 1 : \sqrt{2}$ for sides *AB* : *AC* : *BC* to determine that the multiplier *x* is 5. You then find that the sides of the triangle have lengths $5 : 5 : 5\sqrt{2}$. Therefore, the length of side *AC* = 5, and the length of side *BC* = $5\sqrt{2}$. Using the same figure, though without the information from the previous question, review the following problem:

If the length of side *BC* is $\sqrt{18}$, what are the lengths of sides *AB* and *AC*?

Since the hypotenuse *BC* is $\sqrt{18} = x\sqrt{2}$, solve for *x*: $\sqrt{18} \div \sqrt{2} = \sqrt{9} = 3$. Thus, the sides *AB* and *AC* are each equal to *x*, which is 3.

One reason that the 45–45–90 triangle is so important is that this triangle is exactly half of a square! That is, two 45–45–90 triangles put together make up a square. Thus, if you are given the diagonal of a square, you can use the 45–45–90 ratio to find the length of a side of the square.

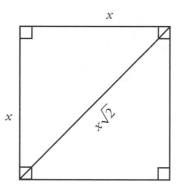

Check Your Skills

19. What is the area of a square with diagonal of 6?
20. What is the diagonal of a square with an area of 25?

Answers can be found on page 64.

Equilateral Triangles and the 30–60–90 Triangle

An equilateral triangle is one in which all three sides (and all three angles) are equal. Each angle of an equilateral triangle is 60° (because all three angles must sum to 180°). A close relative of the equilateral triangle is the 30–60–90 triangle. Notice that two 30–60–90 triangles, when put together, form an equilateral triangle:

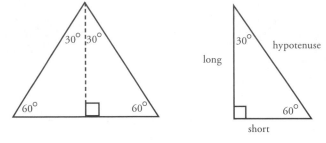

Equilateral Triangle   30–60–90 Triangle

The lengths of the legs of every 30–60–90 triangle have the following ratio, which you must memorize:

30°	→	60°	→	90°
short leg		long leg		hypotenuse
1	:	$\sqrt{3}$	:	**2**
x	:	$x\sqrt{3}$	:	$2x$

> If the short leg of a 30–60–90 triangle has a length of 6, what are the lengths of the long leg and the hypotenuse?

The short leg, which is opposite the 30° angle, is 6. Use the ratio $1 : \sqrt{3} : 2$ to determine that the multiplier x is 6. You then find that the sides of the triangle have lengths $6 : 6\sqrt{3} : 12$. The long leg measures $6\sqrt{3}$ and the hypotenuse measures 12. Try another problem:

> If an equilateral triangle has a side of length 10, what is its height?

Looking at the equilateral triangle on the previous page, you can see that the side of an equilateral triangle is the same as the hypotenuse of a 30–60–90 triangle. Additionally, the height of an equilateral triangle is the same as the long leg of a 30–60–90 triangle.

Since you are told that the hypotenuse is 10, use the ratio $x : x\sqrt{3} : 2x$ to get $2x = 10$ and determine that the multiplier x is 5. You then find that the sides of the 30–60–90 triangle have lengths $5 : 5\sqrt{3} : 10$. Thus, the long leg has a length of $5\sqrt{3}$, which is the height of the equilateral triangle.

If you get tangled up on a 30–60–90 triangle, try to find the length of the short leg. The other legs will then be easier to figure out.

MANHATTAN
PREP

<u>Check Your Skills</u>

21. Quadrilateral *ABCD* (to the right) is composed of four 30–60–90 triangles. If $BD = 10(\sqrt{3})$, what is the perimeter of *ABCD*?

22. Each side of the equilateral triangle below is 2. What is the height *h* of the triangle?

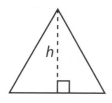

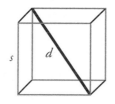

Answers can be found on page 64.

Diagonals of Other Polygons

Right triangles are useful for more than just triangle problems. They are also helpful for finding the diagonals of other polygons, specifically squares, cubes, rectangles, and rectangular solids.

The diagonal of a square can be found using the formula $d = s\sqrt{2}$, where *s* is a side of the square. This is also the diagonal of a face of a cube.

Alternatively, you can recall that any square can be divided into two 45–45–90 triangles, and you can use the ratio $1 : 1 : \sqrt{2}$ to find the diagonal. You can also always use the Pythagorean theorem:

> If a square has a side of length 7, what is the length of the diagonal of the square?

Using the formula $d = s\sqrt{2}$, you find that the length of the diagonal of the square is $7\sqrt{2}$.

The main diagonal of a cube can be found using the formula $d = s\sqrt{3}$, where *s* is an edge of the cube. Try an example:

> What is the measure of an edge of a cube with a main diagonal of length $\sqrt{60}$?

Again, using the formula $d = s\sqrt{3}$, solve as follows:

$$\sqrt{60} = s\sqrt{3} \rightarrow s = \frac{\sqrt{60}}{\sqrt{3}} = \sqrt{20}$$

Thus, the length of the edge of the cube is $\sqrt{20} = 2\sqrt{5}$.

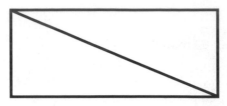

To find the diagonal of a rectangle, you must know EITHER the length and the width OR one dimension and the proportion of one to the other.

Use the rectangle to the left for the next two problems:

If the rectangle above has a length of 12 and a width of 5, what is the length of the diagonal?

Using the Pythagorean theorem, solve:

$$5^2 + 12^2 = c^2 \rightarrow 25 + 144 = c^2 \rightarrow c = 13$$

Thus, the diagonal length is 13.

If the rectangle above has a width of 6, and the ratio of the width to the length is 3 : 4, what is the diagonal?

In this problem, you can use the ratio to find the value of the length. Using the ratio of 3 : 4 given in this problem, you find that the length is 8. Now you can use the Pythagorean theorem. Alternatively, you can recognize that this is a 6–8–10 triangle. Either way, the diagonal length is 10.

Check Your Skills

23. What is the diagonal of the rectangle to the right?

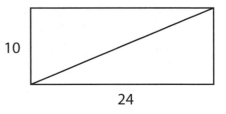

10

24

24. If the rectangle to the right has a perimeter of 6, what is its diagonal?

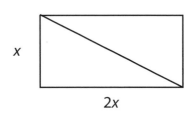

x

2x

Answers can be found on page 64.

Check Your Skills Answer Key

1. **No:** If the two known sides of the triangle are 5 and 19, then the third side of the triangle cannot have a length of 13, because that would violate the rule that any two sides of a triangle must add up to greater than the third side: $5 + 13 = 18$, and $18 < 19$:

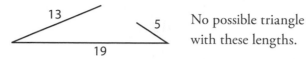

No possible triangle with these lengths.

2. **9 < third side < 25:** If the two known sides of the triangle are 8 and 17, then the third side must be less than the sum of the other two sides: $8 + 17 = 25$, so the third side must be less than 25. The third side must also be greater than the difference of the other two sides: $17 - 8 = 9$, so the third side must be greater than 9. That means that $9 <$ third side < 25.

3. **65°:** The internal angles of a triangle must add up to 180°, so you know that $40 + 75 + x = 180$. Solving for x gives you $x = 65°$:

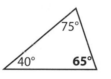

4. **65°:** The three internal angles of the triangle must add up to 180°, so $50 + x + x = 180$. That means that $2x = 130$, and $x = 65$:

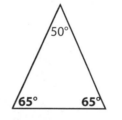

5. **$x = 70°$, $y = 80°$:** In order to determine the missing angles of the triangle, you need to do a little work with the picture. You can figure out the value of x, because straight lines have a degree measure of 180, so $110 + x = 180$, which means $x = 70$. That means your picture looks like this:

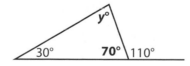

Now you can find y, because $30 + 70 + y = 180$. Solving for y gives you $y = 80$:

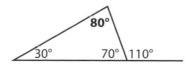

6. **80°:** In this triangle, two sides have the same length, which means this triangle is isosceles. You also know that the two angles opposite the two equal sides will also be equal. That means that *x* must be 80:

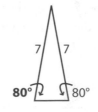

7. **4:** In this triangle, two angles are equal, which means this triangle is isosceles. Thus, you also know that the two sides opposite the equal angles must also be equal, so *x* must equal 4:

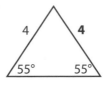

8. **110°:** This triangle is isosceles, because two sides have the same length. That means that the angles opposite the equal sides must also be equal. That means the triangle really looks like this:

Now you can find *x*, because you know 35 + 35 + *x* = 180. Solving for *x* gives you *x* = 110:

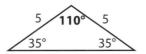

9. **25:**

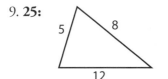

To find the perimeter of the triangle, add up all three sides: 5 + 8 + 12 = 25. Thus, the perimeter is 25.

10. **16:** To find the perimeter of the triangle, you need the lengths of all three sides. This is an isosceles triangle, because two angles are equal. That means that the sides opposite the equal angles must also be equal. So your triangle looks like this:

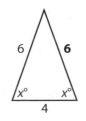

The perimeter is 6 + 6 + 4, which equals 16.

11. **15:** The area of a triangle is $\frac{1}{2} b \times h$. In the triangle shown, the base is 6 and the height is 5, so the area is $\frac{1}{2}(6) \times 5$, which equals 15.

12. **35:** In this triangle, the base is 10 and the height is 7. Remember that the height must be perpendicular to the base—it doesn't need to lie within the triangle. Thus, the area is $\frac{1}{2}(10) \times 7$, which equals 35.

13. **6:** This is a right triangle, so you can use the Pythagorean theorem to solve for the length of the third side. The hypotenuse is the side with length 10, so the formula is $(8)^2 + b^2 = (10)^2$. Thus, $64 + b^2 = 100$, so b^2 is 36, which means $b = 6$. The third side of the triangle has a length of 6. Alternatively, you could recognize that this triangle is one of the Pythagorean triples—a 6–8–10 triangle, which is just a doubled 3–4–5 triangle.

14. **13:** This is a right triangle, so you can use the Pythagorean theorem to solve for the length of the third side. The hypotenuse is the unknown side, so the formula is $(5)^2 + (12)^2 = c^2$. Thus, $25 + 144 = c^2$, so $c^2 = 169$, which means c is 13. The third side of the triangle has a length of 13. Alternatively, you could recognize that this triangle is one of the Pythagorean triples—a 5–12–13 triangle.

15. **6:** This is a right triangle, so you can use the Pythagorean theorem to solve for the third side, or recognize that this is a 3–4–5 triangle. Either way, the result is the same: the length of the third side is 3:

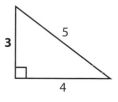

Now you can find the area of the triangle. Area of a triangle is $\frac{1}{2} b \times h$, so the area of this triangle is $\frac{1}{2}(3) \times (4)$, which equals 6.

16. $\sqrt{2}$: Apply the Pythagorean theorem directly, substituting 1 for a and b, and C for c:

$$1^2 + 1^2 = C^2$$
$$2 = C^2$$
$$C = \sqrt{2}$$

17. $\sqrt{3}$: Apply the Pythagorean theorem directly, substituting 1 for a and 2 for c, and B for b:

$$1^2 + B^2 = 2^2$$
$$1 + B^2 = 4$$
$$B^2 = 3$$
$$B = \sqrt{3}$$

18. **3 or 4:** Since an isosceles triangle has two equal sides, the third side must be equal to one of the two named sides.

19. **18:** Call the side length of the square x. Thus, the diagonal would be $x\sqrt{2}$. You know the diagonal is 6, so $x\sqrt{2} = 6$. This means $x = \dfrac{6}{\sqrt{2}}$. The area is $x \times x$, or $\dfrac{6}{\sqrt{2}} \times \dfrac{6}{\sqrt{2}} = \dfrac{36}{2} = 18$.

20. **$5\sqrt{2}$:** If the area is 25, the side length x is 5. Since the diagonal is $x\sqrt{2}$, the diagonal is $5\sqrt{2}$.

21. **40:** The long diagonal BD is the sum of two long legs of the 30–60–90 triangle, so each long leg is $5\sqrt{3}$. The leg : leg : hypotenuse ratio of a 30–60–90 triangle is $x : x\sqrt{3} : 2x$, which means that $5\sqrt{3} = x\sqrt{3}$. Therefore, $x = 5$, so the length of the short leg is 5 and the length of the hypotenuse is 10. Since the perimeter of the figure is the sum of four hypotenuses, the perimeter of this figure is 40.

22. **$\sqrt{3}$:** The line along which the height is measured in the figure bisects the equilateral triangle, creating two identical 30–60–90 triangles, each with a base of 1. The base of each of these triangles is the short leg of a 30–60–90 triangle. Since the leg : leg : hypotenuse ratio of a 30–60–90 triangle is $1 : \sqrt{3} : 2$, the long leg of each 30–60–90 triangle, also the height of the equilateral triangle, is $\sqrt{3}$:

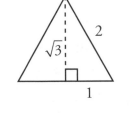

23. **26:** The diagonal of the rectangle is the hypotenuse of a right triangle whose legs are the length and width of the rectangle. In this case, that means that the legs of the right triangle are 10 and 24. Plug these leg lengths into the Pythagorean theorem:

$$a^2 + b^2 = c^2$$
$$10^2 + 24^2 = c^2$$
$$c^2 = 100 + 576 = 676$$
$$c = \sqrt{676} = 26$$

You could use the calculator to take this big square root.

Alternatively, you could recognize the 10 : 24 : 26 triangle (a multiple of the more common 5 : 12 : 13 triangle) and save yourself the trouble.

24. **$\sqrt{5}$:** The perimeter of a rectangle is 2(length + width). In this case, that means $2(x + 2x)$, which equals $6x$. You are told the perimeter equals 6, so $6x = 6$, and x is 1. Therefore, the length ($2x$) is 2 and the width (x) is 1. The diagonal of the rectangle is the hypotenuse of a right triangle whose legs are the length and width of the rectangle. Plug the leg lengths into the Pythagorean theorem:

$$a^2 + b^2 = c^2$$
$$1^2 + 2^2 = c^2$$
$$c^2 = 1 + 4 = 5$$
$$c = \sqrt{5}$$

MANHATTAN
PREP

Problem Set

(Note: Figures are not drawn to scale.)

1. A square is bisected into two equal triangles (see figure to the right). If the length of *BD* is $16\sqrt{2}$ inches, what is the area of the square?

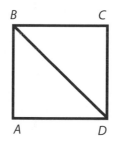

2. Beginning in Town A, Biker Bob rode his bike 10 miles west, 3 miles north, 5 miles east, and then 9 miles north to Town B. How far apart are Town A and Town B? (Assume perfectly flat terrain.)

3. Now in Town B, Biker Bob walked 10 miles due west, and then straight north to Town C. If Town B and Town C are 26 miles apart, how many miles north did he go? (Again, assume perfectly flat terrain.)

4. The longest side of an isosceles right triangle measures $20\sqrt{2}$. What is the area of the triangle?

5. A square field has an area of 400 square meters. Posts are set at all corners of the field. What is the longest distance between any two posts?

6. In triangle *ABC*, *AD* = *BD* = *DC* (see figure to the right). What is *x*?

7. Two sides of a triangle are 4 and 10. If the third side is an integer *x*, how many possible values are there for *x*?

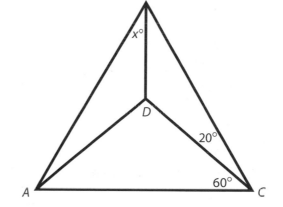

8. Jack has a box in the shape of a cube, the inside edges of which are 4 inches long. What is the longest object he could fit inside the box (i.e., what is the diagonal of the cube)?

9. What is the area of an equilateral triangle whose sides measure 8 cm long?

10. The points of a six-pointed star consist of six identical equilateral triangles, with each side 4 cm (see figure). What is the area of the entire star, including the center?

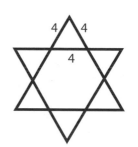

11. What is *x* in the figure below?

12.

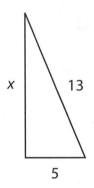

Quantity A	**Quantity B**
x	12

13.

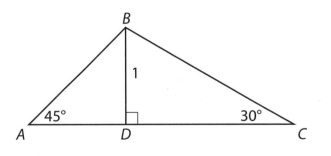

Quantity A	**Quantity B**
The perimeter of triangle ABC	5

MANHATTAN
PREP

14.

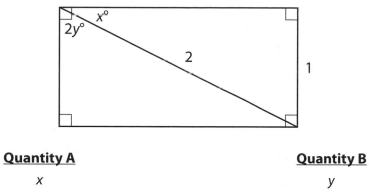

Quantity A	**Quantity B**
x	y

Solutions

1. **256 inches²:** The diagonal of a square is $s\sqrt{2}$; therefore, the side length of square $ABCD$ is 16. The area of the square is s^2, or 16^2, which is 256.

2. **13 miles:** If you draw a rough sketch of the path Biker Bob takes, as shown to the right, you can see that the direct distance from A to B forms the hypotenuse of a right triangle. The short leg (horizontal) is $10 - 5 = 5$ miles, and the long leg (vertical) is $9 + 3 = 12$ miles. Therefore, you can use the Pythagorean theorem to find the direct distance from A to B:

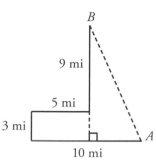

$$5^2 + 12^2 = c^2$$
$$25 + 144 = c^2$$
$$c^2 = 169$$
$$c = 13$$

You might recognize the common right triangle: 5–12–13.

3. **24 miles:** If you draw a rough sketch of the path Biker Bob takes, as shown to the right, you can see that the direct distance from B to C forms the hypotenuse of a right triangle:

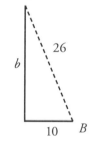

$$10^2 + b^2 = 26^2$$
$$100 + b^2 = 676$$
$$b^2 = 576$$
$$b = 24$$

You might also recognize this as a multiple of the common 5–12–13 triangle.

4. **200:** An isosceles right triangle is a 45–45–90 triangle, with sides in the ratio of $1 : 1 : \sqrt{2}$. If the longest side, the hypotenuse, measures $20\sqrt{2}$, the two other sides each measure 20. Therefore, the area of the triangle is:

$$A = \frac{b \times h}{2} = \frac{20 \times 20}{2} = 200$$

5: **$20\sqrt{2}$ meters:** The longest distance between any two posts is the diagonal of the field. If the area of the square field is 400 square meters, then each side must measure 20 meters. Diagonal is $d = s\sqrt{2}$, so d is $20\sqrt{2}$.

6. 10: If $AD = BD = DC$, then the three triangular regions in this figure are all isosceles triangles. Therefore, you can fill in some of the missing angle measurements as shown below. Since you know that there are 180° in the large triangle ABC, you can write the following equation:

$$x + x + 20 + 20 + 60 + 60 = 180$$
$$2x + 160 = 180$$
$$x = 10$$

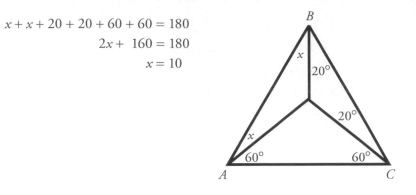

7. 7: If two sides of a triangle are 4 and 10, the third side must be greater than $10 - 4$ and smaller than $10 + 4$. Therefore, the possible values for x are {7, 8, 9, 10, 11, 12, and 13}. You can draw a sketch to convince yourself of this result:

8. $4\sqrt{3}$ inches: The diagonal of a cube with side s is $s\sqrt{3}$. Therefore, the longest object Jack could fit inside the box would be $4\sqrt{3}$ inches long.

9. $16\sqrt{3}$ cm³: Draw in the height of the triangle (see figure). If triangle ABC is an equilateral triangle, and ABD is a right triangle, then ABD is a 30–60–90 triangle. Therefore, its sides are in the ratio of $1 : \sqrt{3} : 2$. If the hypotenuse is 8, then the short leg is 4, and the long leg is $4\sqrt{3}$. This is the height of equilateral triangle ABC. Find the area of triangle ABC with the formula for area of a triangle:

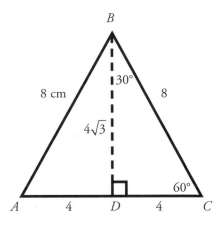

$$A = \frac{b \times h}{2} = \frac{8 \times 4\sqrt{3}}{2} = 16\sqrt{3}$$

10. $48\sqrt{3}$cm²: Think of this star as a large equilateral triangle with sides 12 centimeters long, and three additional smaller equilateral triangles (shaded in the figure below) with sides 4 inches long. Using the same 30–60–90 logic you applied in problem #9, you can see that the height of the larger equilateral triangle is $6\sqrt{3}$, and the height of the smaller equilateral triangle is $2\sqrt{3}$.

MANHATTAN
PREP

Therefore, the areas of the triangles are as follows:

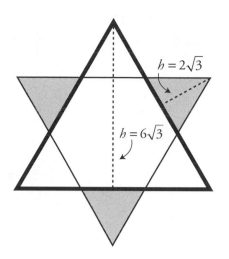

Large triangle: $A = \dfrac{b \times h}{2} = \dfrac{12 \times 6\sqrt{3}}{2} = 36\sqrt{3}$

Small triangles: $A = \dfrac{b \times h}{2} = \dfrac{4 \times 2\sqrt{3}}{2} = 4\sqrt{3}$

The total area of three smaller triangles and one large triangle is:

$$36\sqrt{3} + 3(4\sqrt{3}) = 48\sqrt{3} \ \text{cm}^2$$

11. **36/7:** You can calculate the area of the triangle using the side of length 12 as the base:

$$\frac{1}{2}(12)(3) = 18$$

Next, use the side of length 7 as the base (remember, any side can function as the base, provided that you can find the corresponding height) and write the equation for the area:

$$\frac{1}{2}(7)(x) = 18$$

Now solve for x, the unknown height:

$$7x = 36$$

$$x = \frac{36}{7}$$

You could also solve this problem using the Pythagorean theorem, but the process is *much* harder.

12. **(D):** Although this appears to be a 5 : 12 : 13 triangle, you do not know that it is a right triangle. There is no right angle symbol in the diagram. Remember, don't trust the picture! Below are a couple of possible triangles:

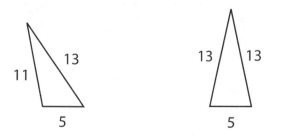

Therefore, **the relationship cannot be determined from the information given**.

13. **(A):** Although there seems to be very little information here, the two small triangles that comprise triangle *ABC* may seem familiar. First, fill in the additional angles in the diagram:

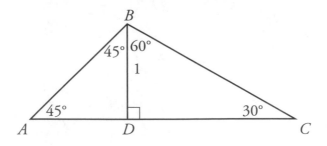

3

With the additional angles filled in, it is clear that the two smaller triangles are special right triangles: a 45–45–90 triangle and a 30–60–90 triangle. You know the ratios of the side lengths for each of these triangles. For a 45–45–90 triangle, the ratio is $x : x : x\sqrt{2}$. In this diagram, the value of x is 1 (side *BD*), so *AD* is 1 and *AB* is $\sqrt{2}$:

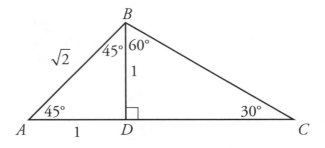

For a 30–60–90 triangle, the ratio is $x : x\sqrt{3} : 2x$. In this diagram, x is 1 (side *BD*), so *DC* is $\sqrt{3}$ and *BC* is 2:

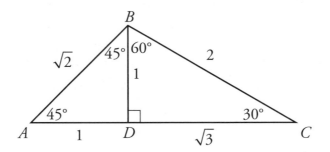

Now calculate the perimeter of triangle *ABC*:

Quantity A	**Quantity B**
The perimeter of triangle *ABC*	5
$= 1 + 2 + \sqrt{2} + \sqrt{3}$	

MANHATTAN
PREP

Now you need to compare this sum to 5. A good approximation of $\sqrt{2}$ is 1.4 and a good approximation of $\sqrt{3}$ is 1.7:

Quantity A	**Quantity B**
$1 + 2 + \sqrt{2} + \sqrt{3} \approx$	5
$1 + 2 + 1.4 + 1.7 = \textbf{6.1}$	

Therefore, **Quantity A is greater**.

Alternatively, you could use the calculator to compute Quantity A.

14. **(C):** The diagonal of the rectangle is the hypotenuse of a right triangle whose legs are the length and width of the rectangle. In this case, you are given the width and the diagonal. Plug these into the Pythagorean theorem to determine the length:

$$a^2 + b^2 = b^2$$
$$1^2 + b^2 = 2^2$$
$$1 + b^2 = 4$$
$$b^2 = 3$$
$$b = \sqrt{3}$$

Label this value on the diagram:

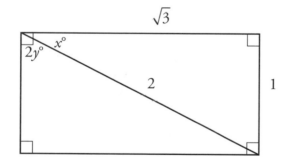

The key to this question is recognizing that each of the triangles is a 30–60–90 triangle. Any time you see a right triangle and one of the sides has a length of $\sqrt{3}$ or a multiple of $\sqrt{3}$, you should check to see whether it is a 30–60–90 triangle. Another clue is a right triangle in which the hypotenuse is twice the length of one of the other sides.

Now, in addition to the side lengths, you can fill in the values of the angles in this diagram. Angle x is opposite the short leg, which means it has a degree measure of 30. Similarly, $2y$ is opposite the long leg, which means it has a degree measure of 60:

$$2y = 60$$
$$y = 30$$

Quantity A	**Quantity B**
$x = 30$	$y = 30$

Therefore, **the two quantities are equal**.

Chapter 4
of Geometry

Polygons

In This Chapter...

Chapter 4
Polygons

Polygons are a very familiar sight on the GRE. As you saw in the last chapter, many questions about triangles will often involve other polygons, most notably quadrilaterals. Mastery of polygons will ultimately involve understanding the basic properties, such as perimeter and area, and will also involve the ability to distinguish certain polygons from other polygons or circles within the context of a larger diagram.

A polygon is defined as a closed shape formed entirely by line segments. The polygons tested on the GRE include the following:

- Three-sided shapes (Triangles)
- Four-sided shapes (Quadrilaterals)
- Other polygons with n sides (where n is five or more)

This section will focus on polygons of four or more sides. In particular, the GRE emphasizes quadrilaterals—four-sided polygons—especially squares, rectangles, parallelograms, and trapezoids.

Polygons are two-dimensional shapes—they lie in a plane. The GRE tests your ability to work with different measurements associated with polygons. The measurements you must be adept with are 1) interior angles, 2) perimeter, and 3) area.

The GRE also tests your knowledge of three-dimensional shapes formed from polygons, particularly rectangular solids and cubes. The measurements you must be adept with are 1) surface area, and 2) volume.

Quadrilaterals: An Overview

The most common polygon tested on the GRE, aside from the triangle, is the quadrilateral (any four-sided polygon). Almost all GRE polygon problems involve the special types of quadrilaterals shown below:

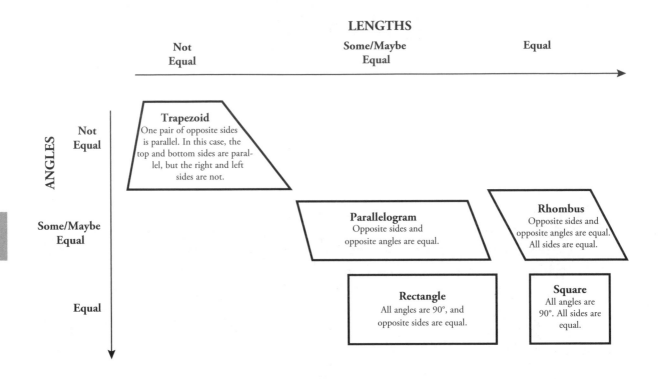

Polygons and Interior Angles

The sum of the interior angles of a given polygon depends on the **number of sides in the polygon**. The following chart displays the relationship between the type of polygon and the sum of its interior angles:

Polygon	# of Sides	Sum of Interior Angles
Triangle	3	180°
Quadrilateral	4	360°
Pentagon	5	540°
Hexagon	6	720°

The sum of the interior angles of a polygon follows a specific pattern that depends on n, the number of sides that the polygon has. This sum is always $(n - 2) \times 180$, because the polygon can be cut into $(n - 2)$ triangles, each of which contains 180°.

$$(n - 2) \times 180 = \text{the SUM of interior angles of a polygon}$$

If you forget this formula, you can always say, "Okay, a triangle has 180°, a rectangle has 360°," and so on. Add 180° for each additional side.

Take a look at the picture below. Since this polygon has four sides, the sum of its interior angles is $(4 - 2)180 = 2(180) = 360°$. Alternatively, note that a quadrilateral can be cut into two triangles by a line connecting opposite corners. Thus, the sum of the angles is 2(180), which equals 360°.

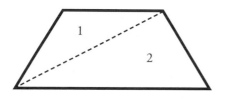

If a polygon has six sides, as in the figure to the right, the sum of its interior angles is $(6 - 2)180 = 4(180) = 720°$.

Alternatively, note that a hexagon can be cut into four triangles by three lines connecting corners. Thus, the sum of the angles is 4(180), which is 720°.

By the way, the corners of polygons are also known as vertices (singular: vertex).

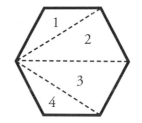

Check Your Skills

1. What is the sum of the interior angles of an octagon (eight-sided polygon)?

2. A regular polygon is a polygon in which every side is of equal length and every interior angle is equal. What is the degree measure of each interior angle in a regular hexagon (six-sided polygon)?

Answers can be found on page 89.

Polygons and Perimeter

The perimeter refers to the distance around a polygon, or the sum of the lengths of all the sides. The amount of fencing needed to surround a yard would be equivalent to the perimeter of that yard (the sum of all the sides).

The perimeter of the pentagon to the right is:

$9 + 7 + 4 + 6 + 5 = \mathbf{31}$

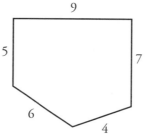

Check Your Skills

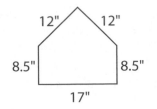

3. The figure above represents a standard baseball home plate. What is the perimeter of this figure?

The answer can be found on page 89.

Polygons and Area

The area of a polygon refers to the space inside the polygon. For example, the amount of space that a garden occupies is the area of that garden. Area is measured in square units, such as cm² (square centimeters), m² (square meters), or ft² (square feet).

On the GRE, there are two polygon area formulas you **must** know:

1. Area of a Triangle $= \dfrac{\textbf{Base} \times \textbf{Height}}{\textbf{2}}$

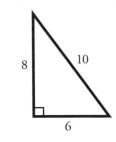

The height *always* refers to a line that is perpendicular (at a 90° angle) to the base.

In this triangle, the base is 6 and the height (perpendicular to the base) is 8. Thus, the area is $(6 \times 8) \div 2 = 48 \div 2 = 24$.

2. Area of a Rectangle $= \textbf{Length} \times \textbf{Width}$

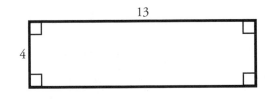

The length of this rectangle is 13, and the width is 4. Therefore, the area is $13 \times 4 = 52$.

The GRE will occasionally ask you to find the area of a polygon more comp~~l~~ rectangle. The following formulas can be used to find the areas of other typ

3. Area of a Trapezoid $= \dfrac{(\textbf{Base}_1 + \textbf{Base}_2)}{\textbf{2}} \times \textbf{Height}$

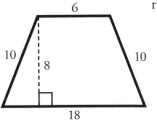

Note that the height refers to a line perpendicular to the two bases, which are parallel. (You often have to draw in the height, as in this case.)

In the trapezoid shown, base$_1$ = 18, base$_2$ = 6, and the height = 8.

Thus, the area is $\frac{(18+6)}{2} \times 8 = 96$. Another way to think about this is to take the *average* of the two bases and multiply it by the height.

4. Area of any Parallelogram = **Base × Height**

Note that the height refers to the line perpendicular to the base. (As with the trapezoid, you often have to draw in the height.) In the parallelogram shown, the base = 5 and the height = 8. Therefore, the area is 5 × 8, which is 40.

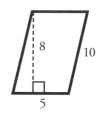

Although these formulas are very useful to memorize for the GRE, you may notice that all of the shapes to the right can actually be divided into some combination of rectangles and right triangles. Therefore, if you forget the area formula for a particular shape, simply cut the shape into rectangles and right triangles, and then find the areas of these individual pieces. For example:

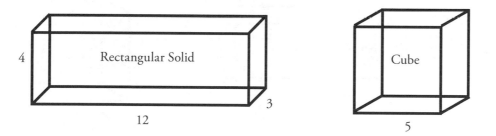

3 Dimensions: Surface Area

The GRE tests two particular three-dimensional shapes formed from polygons: the rectangular solid and the cube. Note that a cube is just a special type of rectangular solid:

The surface area of a three-dimensional shape is the amount of space on the surface of that particular object. For example, the amount of paint that it would take to fully cover a rectangular box could be determined by finding the surface area of that box. As with simple area, surface area is measured in square units such as in^2 (square inches) or ft^2 (square feet).

> **Surface Area = the SUM of the areas of ALL of the faces**

Both a rectangular solid and a cube have **six faces**.

To determine the surface area of a rectangular solid, you must find the area of each face. Notice, however, that in a rectangular solid, the front and back faces have the same area, the top and bottom faces have the same area, and the two side faces have the same area. In the rectangular solid, the area of the front face is equal to $12 \times 4 = 48$. Thus, the back face also has an area of 48. The area of the bottom face is equal to $12 \times 3 = 36$. Thus, the top face also has an area of 36. Finally, each side face has an area of $3 \times 4 = 12$. Therefore, the surface area, or the sum of the areas of all six faces, is: $48(2) + 36(2) + 12(2) = 192$.

To determine the surface area of a cube, you only need the length of one side. You can see from the cube above that a cube is made of six identical square surfaces. First, find the area of one face: $5 \times 5 = 25$. Then, multiply by 6 to account for all of the faces: $25 \times 6 = 150$.

Check Your Skills

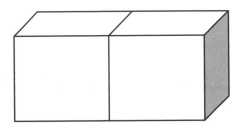

4. The figure to the left shows two wooden cubes joined to form a rectangular solid. If each cube has a surface area of 24, what is the surface area of the resulting rectangular solid?

The answer can be found on page 89.

3 Dimensions: Volume

The volume of a three-dimensional shape is the amount of "stuff" it can hold. For example, the amount of liquid that a rectangular milk carton holds can be determined by finding the volume of the carton. Volume is measured in cubic units such as in³ (cubic inches) or ft³ (cubic feet).

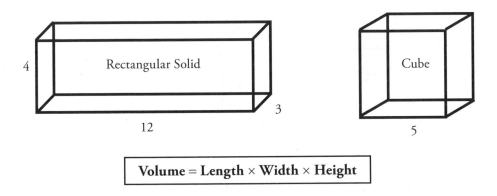

$$\boxed{\textbf{Volume} = \textbf{Length} \times \textbf{Width} \times \textbf{Height}}$$

By looking at the rectangular solid above, you can see that the length is 12, the width is 3, and the height is 4. Therefore, the volume is $12 \times 3 \times 4$, which is 144.

In a cube, all three of the dimensions—length, width, and height—are identical. Therefore, knowing the measurement of just one side of the cube is sufficient to find the volume. In the cube above, the volume is $5 \times 5 \times 5$, which equals 125.

Check Your Skills

5. The volume of a rectangular solid with length 8, width 6, and height 4 is how many times the volume of a rectangular solid with length 4, width 3, and height 2?

The answer can be found on page 89.

Quadrilaterals

A quadrilateral is any figure with four sides. The GRE largely deals with one class of quadrilaterals known as **parallelograms**. A parallelogram is any four-sided figure in which the opposite sides are parallel and equal and in which opposite angles are equal. This is an example of a parallelogram:

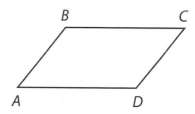

In this figure, sides *AB* and *CD* are parallel and have equal lengths, sides *AD* and *BC* are parallel and have equal lengths, angles *ADC* and *ABC* are equal, and angles *BAD* and *BCD* are equal:

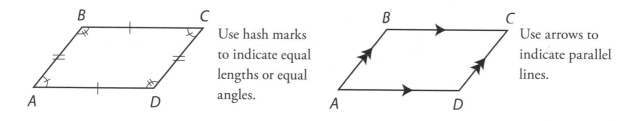

Use hash marks to indicate equal lengths or equal angles.

Use arrows to indicate parallel lines.

Any quadrilateral with two sets of opposite and equal sides is a parallelogram, as is any quadrilateral with two sets of opposite and equal angles.

An additional property of any parallelogram is that the diagonal will divide the parallelogram into two equal triangles:

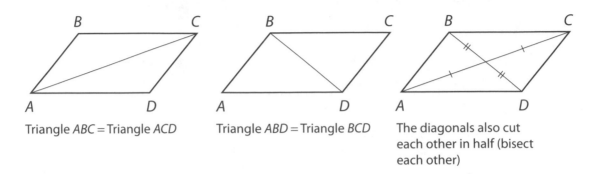

Triangle *ABC* = Triangle *ACD*   Triangle *ABD* = Triangle *BCD*   The diagonals also cut
each other in half (bisect
each other)

For any parallelogram, the perimeter is the sum of the lengths of all the sides and the area is equal to (base) × (height). With parallelograms, as with triangles, it is important to remember that the base and the height *must* be perpendicular to one another.

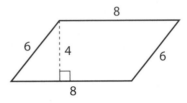

In the parallelogram above, what is the perimeter, and what is the area? The perimeter is the sum of the sides, so it is equal to 6 + 8 + 6 + 8, which is 28. Alternatively, you can use one of the properties of parallelograms to calculate the perimeter in a different way. You know that parallelograms have two sets of equal sides. In this parallelogram, two of the sides have a length of 6, and two of the sides have a length of 8. So the perimeter equals 2 × 6 + 2 × 8. You can factor out a 2, and say that perimeter is 2 × (6 + 8), which equals 28.

To calculate the area, you need a base and a height. It might be tempting to say that the area is 8 × 6 = 48. But the two sides of this parallelogram are not perpendicular to each other. The dotted line drawn into the figure, however, is perpendicular to the base. The area of the parallelogram is 8 × 4 = 32.

<u>Check Your Skills</u>

6. What is the perimeter of the parallelogram?

7. What is the area of the parallelogram?

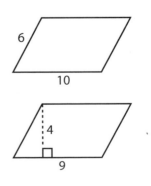

Answers can be found on pages 89–90.

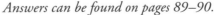

Rectangles

Rectangles are a specific type of parallelogram. Rectangles have all the same properties as parallelograms, with one additional property—all four internal angles of a rectangle are right angles. Additionally, with rectangles, one pair of sides is referred to as the length and one pair of sides as the width.

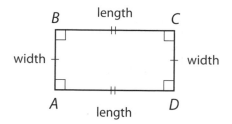

The formula for the perimeter of a rectangle is the same as for the perimeter of a parallelogram—either sum the lengths of the four sides or add the length and the width then multiply by 2.

The formula for the area of a rectangle is also the same as for the area of a parallelogram, but for any rectangle, the length and width are by definition perpendicular to each other, so you don't need a separate height. For this reason, the area of a rectangle is commonly expressed as (length) × (width).

Here's practice. For the following rectangle, find the perimeter and the area:

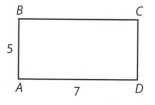

Start with the perimeter. Again, recognize that you have two sides with a length of 5 and two sides with a length of 7. Therefore, the perimeter is 2 × (5 + 7), which equals 24. Or, just add the sides up; 5 + 5 + 7 + 7 also equals 24.

Now to find the area. The formula for area is (length) × (width). For the purposes of finding the area, it is irrelevant which side is the length and which side is the width. If you make side *AB* the length and side *AD* the width, then the area = (5) × (7) = 35. If, instead, you make side *AD* the length and side *AB* the width, then you have area = (7) × (5) = 35. The only thing that matters is that you choose two sides that are perpendicular to each other.

Check Your Skills

Find the area and perimeter of each rectangle.

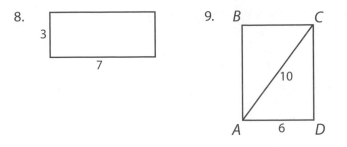

Answers can be found on page 90.

Squares

One particular type of rectangle warrants mention—the square. Everything that is true of rectangles is true of squares as well. However, a square is a rectangle in which the lengths of all four sides are equal. Thus, knowing only one side of a square is enough to determine the perimeter and area of a square.

For instance, if you have a square, and you know that the length of one of its sides is 3, you know that all four sides have a length of 3:

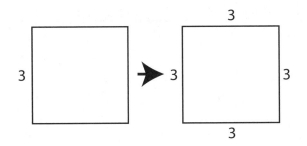

The perimeter of the square is $3 + 3 + 3 + 3$, which equals 12. Alternatively, once you know the length of one side of a square, you can multiply that length by 4 to find the perimeter: $3 \times 4 = 12$.

To find the area, use the same formula as for a rectangle: Area = (length) × (width). But, because the shape is a square, you know that the length and the width are equal. Therefore, you can say that the area of a square is Area = (side)^2. In this case, Area = $(3)^2 = 9$.

Maximum Area of Polygons

In some problems, the GRE may require you to determine the maximum or minimum area of a given figure. Following a few simple shortcuts can help you solve certain problems quickly.

MANHATTAN
PREP

Maximum Area of a Quadrilateral

Perhaps the best-known maximum area problem is one that asks you to maximize the area of a *quadrilateral* (usually a rectangle) with a *fixed perimeter*. If a quadrilateral has a fixed perimeter, say, 36 inches, it can take a variety of shapes:

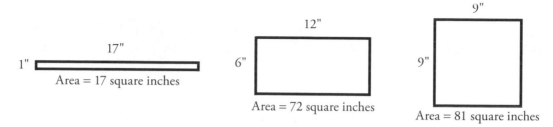

Of these figures, the one with the largest area is the square. This is a general rule: **Of all quadrilaterals with a given perimeter, the *square* has the largest area.** This is true even in cases involving non-integer lengths. For instance, of all quadrilaterals with a perimeter of 25 feet, the one with the largest area is a square with $25 \div 4 = 6.25$ feet per side.

This principle can also be turned around to yield the following corollary: **Of all quadrilaterals with a given area, the *square* has the minimum perimeter.**

Both of these principles can be generalized for polygons with n sides: **A regular polygon with all sides equal and all angles equal will maximize area for a given perimeter and minimize perimeter for a given area.**

Maximum Area of a Parallelogram or Triangle

Another common optimization problem involves maximizing the area of a *triangle or parallelogram with given side lengths.*

For instance, there are many triangles with two sides 3 and 4 units long. Imagine that the two sides of lengths 3 and 4 are on a hinge. The third side can have various lengths:

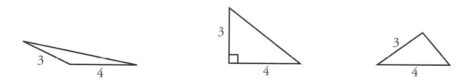

There are many corresponding parallelograms with two sides 3 and 4 units long:

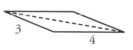
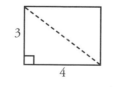
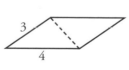

The area of a triangle is given by $A = \frac{1}{2}bh$, and the area of a parallelogram is given by $A = bh$. Because both of these formulas involve the perpendicular height h, the maximum area of each figure is achieved when the 3-unit side is perpendicular to the 4-unit side, so that the height is 3 units. All the other figures have lesser heights. (Note that in this case, the triangle of maximum area is the famous 3–4–5 right triangle.) If the sides are not perpendicular, then the figure is squished, so to speak.

The general rule is this: **If you are given two sides of a triangle or parallelogram, you can maximize the area by placing those two sides PERPENDICULAR to each other.**

4

Check Your Skills Answer Key

1. **1,080°:** One way to calculate the sum of the interior angles of a polygon is by applying the formula $(n - 2)180 =$ Sum of the interior angles, where n is the number of sides. Substituting 8 for n yields:

Sum of the interior angles $= (8 - 2)180$
$$= (6)180$$
$$= 1,080$$

2. **120°:** Since each interior angle is the same, you can determine the angle of any one by dividing the sum of the interior angles by 6 (the number of interior angles). Use the formula $(n - 2)180 =$ Sum of the interior angles, where n is the number of sides. Substituting 6 for n yields: $(4)180 = 720$. Divide 720 by 6 to get 120.

3. **58":** It is simplest to sum the sides in this order: $12 + 12 + 17 + (8^1/2 + 8^1/2) = 12 + 12 + 17 + 17 = 58$.

4. **40:** Since the surface area of a cube is 6 times the area of one face, each square face of each cube must have an area of 4. One face of each cube is lost when the two cubes are joined, so the total surface area of the figure will be the sum of the surface areas of both cubes minus the surface areas of the covered faces.

Each cube has surface area of 24, so the total surface area is 48. Subtract the surface area of each of the two touching (and thus non-exterior) faces: $48 - 2(4) = 40$.

Alternatively, you could find that, because the surface area of one side of each cube is 4, the side length of each cube is 2. Thus, the length of the overall rectangular solid is 4, while its width is 2 and its height is 2. The surface area will now be equal to the sum of all six faces: $2(2 \times 4) + 2(2 \times 4) + 2(2 \times 2) = 40$.

5. **8:** The volume of a rectangular solid is the product of its three dimensions: length, width, and height:

$$8 \times 6 \times 4 = 192 \text{ and } 4 \times 3 \times 2 = 24$$

$\dfrac{192}{24} = 8$, so the volume of the larger solid is 8 times the volume of the smaller solid.

Alternatively, note that each dimension of the larger solid is 2 times the corresponding dimension of the smaller solid. The volume will be 2 times × 2 times × 2 times = 8 times greater.

6. **32:** In parallelograms, opposite sides have equal lengths, so you know that two of the sides of the parallelogram have a length of 6 and two of the sides have a length of 10.

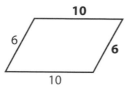

Thus, the perimeter is $6 + 10 + 6 + 10$, which equals 32. Alternatively, $2(6 + 10) = 32$.

7. **36:** Area of a parallelogram is $b \times h$. In this parallelogram, the base is 9 and the height is 4, so the area is 9×4, which equals 36. The area of the parallelogram is 36.

8. **Area = 21, Perimeter = 20:** In rectangles, opposite sides have equal lengths, so your rectangle looks like this:

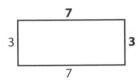

The perimeter is $3 + 7 + 3 + 7$, which equals 20. The area of a rectangle is $l \times w$, so the area is 7×3, which equals 21. The area is 21, and the perimeter is 20.

9. **Area = 48, Perimeter = 28:** To find the area and perimeter of the rectangle, you need to know the length of either side *AB* or side *CD*. The diagonal of the rectangle creates a right triangle, so you can use the Pythagorean theorem to find the length of side *CD*. Alternatively, you can recognize that triangle *ACD* is a 6–8–10 triangle, and thus the length of side *CD* is 8. Either way, your rectangle now looks like this:

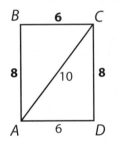

Thus, the perimeter of the rectangle is $6 + 8 + 6 + 8$, which equals 28, and the area is 6×8, which equals 48.

MANHATTAN
PREP

Problem Set

(Note: Figures are not drawn to scale.)

1. Frank the Fencemaker needs to fence in a rectangular yard. He fences in the entire yard, except for one 40-foot side of the yard. The yard has an area of 280 square feet. How many feet of fence does Frank use?

2. A pentagon has three sides with length x, and two sides with the length $3x$. If x is $\frac{2}{3}$ of an inch, what is the perimeter of the pentagon?

3. $ABCD$ is a quadrilateral, with AD parallel to BC (see figure). E is a point between A and D such that BE represents the height of $ABCD$ and E is the midpoint of AD. If the area of triangle ABE is 12.5 square inches, what is the area of $ABCD$?

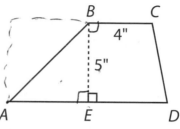

4. A rectangular tank needs to be coated with insulation. The tank has dimensions of 4 feet, 5 feet, and 2.5 feet. Each square foot of insulation costs $20. How much will it cost to cover the surface of the tank with insulation?

5. Triangle ABC (see figure) has a base of $2y$, a height of y, and an area of 49. What is y?

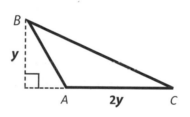

6. 40 percent of Andrea's living room floor is covered by a carpet that is 4 feet by 9 feet. What is the area of her living room floor?

7. If the perimeter of a rectangular flower bed is 30 feet, and its area is 44 square feet, what is the length of each of its shorter sides?

8. There is a rectangular parking lot with a length of $2x$ and a width of x. What is the ratio of the perimeter of the parking lot to the area of the parking lot, in terms of x?

9. A rectangular solid has a square base, with each side of the base measuring 4 meters. If the volume of the solid is 112 cubic meters, what is the surface area of the solid?

10. A swimming pool has a length of 30 meters, a width of 10 meters, and an average depth of 2 meters. If a hose can fill the pool at a rate of 0.5 cubic meters per minute, how many hours will it take the hose to fill the pool?

11. A solid cube has an edge of length 5. What is the ratio of the cube's surface area to its volume?

12. If the length of an edge of cube A is one-third the length of an edge of cube B, what is the ratio of the volume of cube A to the volume of cube B?

13. *ABCD* is a square picture frame (see figure). *EFGH* is a square centered within *ABCD* as a space for a picture. The area of *EFGH* (for the picture) is equal to the area of the picture frame (the area of *ABCD* minus the area of *EFGH*). If *AB* = 6, what is the length of *EF*?

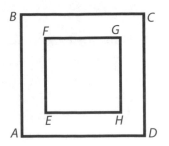

14. What is the maximum possible area of a quadrilateral with a perimeter of 80 centimeters?

15. What is the minimum possible perimeter of a quadrilateral with an area of 1,600 square feet?

16. What is the maximum possible area of a parallelogram with one side of length 2 meters and a perimeter of 24 meters?

17. What is the maximum possible area of a triangle with a side of length 7 units and another side of length 8 units?

18. The lengths of the two shorter legs of a right triangle add up to 40 units. What is the maximum possible area of the triangle?

19.   **Quantity A**   **Quantity B**
      The surface area, in square inches,   The volume, in cubic inches, of
        of a cube with edges of length 6   a cube with edges of length 6

20.   **Quantity A**   **Quantity B**
       The total volume of 3 cubes with   The total volume of 2 cubes with
            edges of length 2   edges of length 3

MANHATTAN
PREP

21.

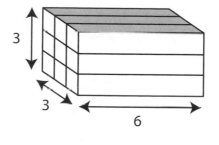

The large rectangular solid
above is formed by binding
together nine identical rectangular rods, as shown.

Quantity A

The combined surface area of
four of the individual, identical
rectangular rods

Quantity B

The surface area of the large
rectangular solid

4

Solutions

1. **54 ft:** You know that one side of the yard is 40 feet long, so call this the length. You also know that the area of the yard is 280 square feet. In order to determine the perimeter, you must know the width of the yard:

$$A = l \times w$$
$$280 = 40w$$
$$w = 280 \div 40 = 7 \text{ feet}$$

Frank fences the two 7-foot sides and one of the 40-foot sides. Therefore, he needs $40 + 2(7) = 54$ feet of fence.

2. **6 inches:** The perimeter of a pentagon is the sum of its five sides: $x + x + x + 3x + 3x = 9x$. If x is $\frac{2}{3}$ of an inch, the perimeter is $9 \times \frac{2}{3}$, or 6 inches.

3. **35 in²:** If E is the midpoint of AD, then $AE = ED$. Set x as the length of each AE and ED. You can determine the length of x by using what you know about the area of triangle ABE:

$$\text{Area} = \frac{b \times h}{2}$$
$$12.5 = \frac{5x}{2}$$
$$25 = 5x$$
$$x = 5$$

Therefore, the length of AD is $2x$, or 10.

Because AD is parallel to BC, the shape $ABCD$ is a trapezoid.

To find the area of the trapezoid, use the formula: $A = \dfrac{b_1 + b_2}{2} \times h$

$$= \frac{4 + 10}{2} \times 5$$
$$= 35 \text{ in}^2$$

4. **$1,700:** To find the surface area of a rectangular solid, sum the individual areas of all six faces:

	Each		Both	
Top and Bottom:	$5 \times 4 = 20$	→	2×20	$= 40$
Side 1:	$5 \times 2.5 = 12.5$	→	2×12.5	$= 25$
Side 2:	$4 \times 2.5 = 10$	→	2×10	$= 20$

$$40 + 25 + 20 - 85 \text{ ft}^2$$

Covering the entire tank will cost $85 \times \$20$, which equals $1,700.

5. **7:** The area of a triangle is equal to half the base times the height. Therefore, you can write the following relationship:

$$\frac{2y(y)}{2} = 49$$

$$y^2 = 49$$

$$y = 7$$

6. **90 ft²:** The area of the carpet is equal to $l \times w$, or 36 ft². Set up a percent table or a proportion to find the area of the whole living room floor:

$$\frac{40}{100} = \frac{36}{x} \qquad \text{Cross-multiply to solve.}$$

$$40x = 3600$$

$$x = 90 \text{ ft}^2$$

7. **4 ft:** Set up equations to represent the area and perimeter of the flower bed:

$$A = l \times w \qquad\qquad\qquad P = 2(l + w)$$

Then, substitute the known values for the variables A and P:

$$44 = l \times w \qquad\qquad\qquad 30 = 2(l + w)$$

Solve the two equations using the substitution method:

$$l = \frac{44}{w}$$

$$30 = 2\left(\frac{44}{w} + w\right)$$

$$30 = \frac{88}{w} + 2w \qquad\qquad \text{Multiply the entire equation by } \frac{w}{2}.$$

$$15w = 44 + w^2$$

$$w^2 - 15w + 44 = 0$$

$$(w - 11)(w - 4) = 0 \qquad\qquad \text{Solving the quadratic equation yields two solutions: 4 and 11.}$$

$$w = \{4,\ 11\} \qquad\qquad \text{Since you are looking only for the length of the shorter side, the answer is 4.}$$

Alternatively, you can arrive at the correct solution by picking numbers. What length and width add up to 15 (half of the perimeter) and multiply to produce 44 (the area)? Some experimentation will demonstrate that the longer side must be 11 and the shorter side must be 4.

MANHATTAN
PREP

8. $\dfrac{3}{x}$: If the length of the parking lot is $2x$ and the width is x, you can set up a fraction to represent the

ratio of the perimeter to the area as follows:

$$\frac{\text{perimeter}}{\text{area}} = \frac{2(2x + x)}{(2x)(x)} = \frac{6x}{2x^2} = \frac{3}{x}$$

9. **144 m²:** The volume of a rectangular solid equals (length) × (width) × (height). If you know that the length and width are both 4 meters long, you can substitute values into the formulas as shown:

$$112 = 4 \times 4 \times h$$
$$h = 7$$

To find the surface area of a rectangular solid, sum the individual areas of all six faces:

	Each		Both
Top and Bottom:	$4 \times 4 = 16$	→	$2 \times 16 = 32$
Side 1:	$4 \times 7 = 28$	→	$2 \times 28 = 56$
Side 2:	$4 \times 7 = 28$	→	$2 \times 28 = 56$

$$32 + 56 + 56 = 144 \text{ m}^2$$

10. **20 hours:** The volume of the pool is (length) × (width) × (height), or $30 \times 10 \times 2 = 600$ cubic meters. Use a standard work equation, $RT = W$, where W represents the total work of 600 m³:

$$0.5t = 600$$
$$t = 1{,}200 \text{ minutes} \quad \text{Convert this time to hours by dividing by 60: } 1{,}200 \div 60 = 20 \text{ hours.}$$

11. $\dfrac{6}{5}$: To find the surface area of a cube, find the area of one face, and multiply that by 6: $6(5^2) = 150$.

To find the volume of a cube, cube its edge length: $5^3 = 125$.

The ratio of the cube's surface area to its volume, therefore, is $\dfrac{150}{125}$, which simplifies to $\dfrac{6}{5}$.

12. $\dfrac{1}{27}$: First, assign the variable x to the length of one side of cube A. Then the length of one side of

cube B is $3x$. The volume of cube A is x^3. The volume of cube B is $(3x)^3$, or $27x^3$.

Therefore, the ratio of the volume of cube A to cube B is $\dfrac{x^3}{27x^3}$, or $\dfrac{1}{27}$. You can also pick

a number for the length of a side of cube A and solve accordingly.

13. **$3\sqrt{2}$:** The area of the frame and the area of the picture sum to the total area of the image, which is 6^2, or 36. Therefore, the area of the frame and the picture are each equal to half of 36, or 18. Since $EFGH$ is a square, the length of EF is $\sqrt{18}$, or $3\sqrt{2}$.

4

14. **400 cm²:** The quadrilateral with maximum area for a given perimeter is a square, which has four equal sides. Therefore, the square that has a perimeter of 80 centimeters has sides of length 20 centimeters each. Since the area of a square is the side length squared, the area = (20 cm)(20 cm) = 400 cm².

15. **160 ft:** The quadrilateral with minimum perimeter for a given area is a square. Since the area of a square is the side length squared, you can solve the equation $x^2 = 1,600 \text{ ft}^2$ for the side length x, yielding $x = 40$ ft. The perimeter, which is four times the side length, is (4)(40 ft) = 160 ft.

16. **20 m²:** If one side of the parallelogram is 2 meters long, then the opposite side must also be 2 meters long. You can solve for the unknown sides, which are equal in length, by writing an equation for the perimeter: $24 = 2(2) + 2x$, with x as the unknown side. Solving, you get $x = 10$ meters. The parallelogram with these dimensions and maximum area is a *rectangle* with 2-meter and 10-meter sides. Thus, the maximum possible area of the figure is (2 m)(10 m) = 20 m².

17. **28 square units:** A triangle with two given sides has maximum area if these two sides are placed at right angles to each other. For this triangle, one of the given sides can be considered the base, and the other side can be considered the height (because they meet at a right angle). Thus, plug these sides into the formula $A = \dfrac{1}{2}bh$: $A = \dfrac{1}{2}(7)(8) = 28$.

18. **200 square units:** You can think of a right triangle as half of a rectangle. Constructing this right triangle with legs adding to 40 is equivalent to constructing the rectangle with a perimeter of 80. Since the area of the triangle is half that of the rectangle, you can use the previously mentioned technique for maximizing the area of a rectangle: of all rectangles with a given perimeter, the *square* has the greatest area. Likewise, of all right triangles with a given perimeter, the isoceles right triangle (a 45–45–90 triangle) has the greatest area. The desired rectangle is thus a 20 by 20 square, and the right triangle has an area of $\dfrac{1}{2}(20)(20) = 200$ units.

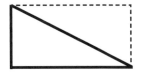

19. **(C):** The surface area of a cube is 6 times e^2, where e is the length of each edge (that is, the surface area is the number of faces times the area of each face). Apply this formula to Quantity A:

Quantity A	**Quantity B**
The surface area, in square inches, of a cube with edges of length 6 = **6 × (6 × 6)**	The volume, in cubic inches, of a cube with edges of length 6

The volume of a cube is e^3, where e is the length of each edge. Apply this formula to Quantity B:

Quantity A	**Quantity B**
6 × (6 × 6)	The volume, in cubic inches, of a cube with edges of length 6 = **6 × 6 × 6**

It is not generally the case that the volume of a cube in cubic units is equal to the surface area of the cube in square inches; they are only equal when the edge of the cube is of length 6. In this case, **the two quantities are equal**.

20. **(B):** The volume of a cube is e^3, where e is the length of each edge. Apply this formula to each quantity:

<table>
<tr><td align="center"><u>Quantity A</u></td><td align="center"><u>Quantity B</u></td></tr>
<tr><td align="center">The total volume of 3 cubes with
edges of length 2 =
$3 \times 2^3 = \mathbf{24}$</td><td align="center">The total volume of 2 cubes
with edges of length 3 =
$2 \times 3^3 = \mathbf{54}$</td></tr>
</table>

Therefore, **Quantity B is greater**.

21. **(A):** A rectangular solid has three pairs of opposing equal faces, each pair representing two of the dimensions of the solid (length × width; length × height; height × width). The total surface area of a rectangular solid is the sum of the surface areas of those three pairs of opposing sides.

According to the diagram, the dimensions of each rod must be 1 × 1 × 6. So each of the rods described in Quantity A has a surface area of:

$$2(1 \times 1) + 2(1 \times 6) + 2(1 \times 6) = 26 \quad \text{or} \quad 2[(1 \times 1) + (1 \times 6) + (1 \times 6)] = 26$$

That is, each rod has a total surface area of 26, and the four rods together have a surface area of 4 × 26 = 104.

<table>
<tr><td align="center"><u>Quantity A</u></td><td align="center"><u>Quantity B</u></td></tr>
<tr><td align="center">The combined surface area of four
of the identical rectangular rods = **104**</td><td align="center">The surface area of the large
rectangular solid</td></tr>
</table>

The large rectangular solid has a total surface area of: 2(3 × 3) + 2(3 × 6) + 2(3 × 6), or 90.

<table>
<tr><td align="center"><u>Quantity A</u></td><td align="center"><u>Quantity B</u></td></tr>
<tr><td align="center">104</td><td align="center">The surface area of the large
rectangular solid = **90**</td></tr>
</table>

Therefore, **Quantity A is greater**.

Chapter 5 *of* Geometry

Circles & Cylinders

In This Chapter...

Chapter 5

Circles & Cylinders

The Basic Elements of a Circle

A circle is a set of points that are all the same distance from a central point. By definition, every circle has a center. Although the center is not itself a point on the circle, it is nevertheless an important component of the circle. The **radius** of a circle is defined as the distance between the center of the circle and a point on the circle. The first thing to know about radii is that *any* line segment connecting the center of the circle (usually labeled O) and *any* point on the circle is a radius (usually labeled r). All radii in the same circle have the same length:

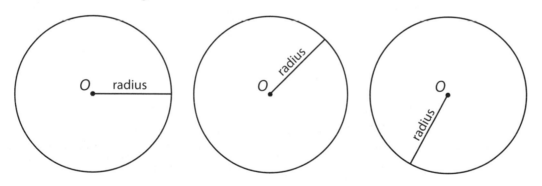

You will review the other basic elements by dealing with a particular circle. Your circle will have a radius of 7, like the one shown below, and you'll see what else you can figure out about the circle based on that one measurement. As you'll see, you'll be able to figure out quite a lot.

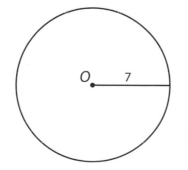

Once you know the radius, the next easiest piece to figure out is the **diameter**. The **diameter** passes through the center of a circle and connects two opposite points on the circle:

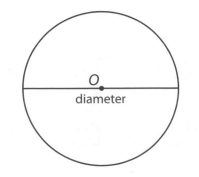

One way of thinking about the diameter (usually referred to as d) is that it is 2 radii laid end to end. The diameter will always be exactly twice the length of the radius. This relationship can be expressed as $d = 2r$. That means that your circle with radius 7 has a diameter of 14.

Now it's time for the next important measurement—the **circumference**. Circumference (usually referred to as C) is a measure of the distance around a circle. One way to think about circumference is that it's the perimeter of a circle:

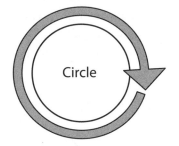

As it happens, there is a consistent relationship between the circumference and the diameter of any circle. If you were to divide the circumference by the diameter, you would always get the same number—3.14 ... (the number is actually a non-terminating decimal, so it's usually rounded to the hundredths place). You may be more familiar with this number as the Greek letter π (pi). To recap:

$$\frac{\text{circumference}}{\text{diameter}} = \pi \qquad\qquad \text{OR} \qquad\qquad \pi d = C$$

In your circle with a diameter of 14, the circumference is $\pi(14) = 14\pi$. The vast majority of questions that involve circles and π will use the Greek letter rather than the decimal approximation for π. Suppose a question about your circle with radius 7 asked for the circumference. The correct answer would read 14π, rather than 43.96 (which is 14×3.14). It's worth mentioning that another very common way of expressing the circumference is that twice the radius times π also equals C, because the diameter is twice the radius. This relationship is commonly expressed as $C = 2\pi r$. As you prepare for the GRE, you should be comfortable using either equation.

MANHATTAN
PREP

There is one more element of a circle that you'll need to be familiar with, and that is **area**. The area (usually referred to as *A*) is the space inside the circle:

Once again, it turns out that there is a consistent relationship between the area of a circle and its diameter (and radius). The formula for the area of a circle is $A = \pi r^2$. For your circle of radius 7, the area is $\pi(7)^2 = 49\pi$. To recap, once you know the radius, you are able to determine the diameter, the circumference, and the area:

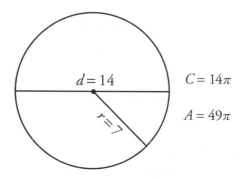

These relationships are true of any circle. What's more, if you know *any* of these values, you can determine the rest. In fact, the ability to use one element of a circle to determine another element is one of the most important skills for answering questions about circles. To review:

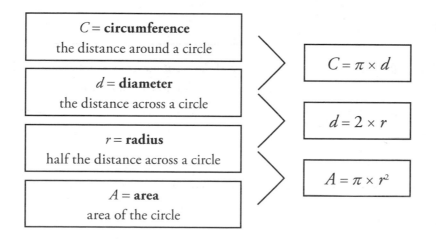

To demonstrate, you'll work through another circle, but this time you know that the area of the circle is 36π. Using the formula for the area, start by plugging this value into it:

$36\pi = \pi r^2$

Now, solve for the radius by isolating r:

$36\pi = \pi r^2$ Divide both sides by π.
$36 = r^2$ Take the square root of both sides.
$6 = r$

Now that you know the radius, you can multiply it by 2 to get the diameter, so your diameter is 6×2, which is 12. Finally, to find the circumference, multiply the diameter by π, which gives you a circumference of 12π:

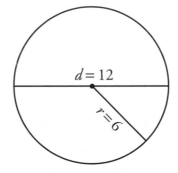

Check Your Skills

1. The radius of a circle is 7. What is the area?
2. The circumference of a circle is 17π. What is the diameter?
3. The area of a circle is 25π. What is the circumference?

Answers can be found on page 113.

Sectors

Continue working with your circle that has an area of 36π. But now, cut it in half and make it a semi-circle. Any time you have a fractional portion of a circle, it's known as a **sector**:

What effect does cutting the circle in half have on the basic elements of the circle? The diameter stays the same, as does the radius. But what happened to the area and the circumference? They're also cut in half. So the area of the semicircle is 18π and the remaining circumference is 6π. When dealing with sectors, the portion of the circumference that remains is called the **arc length**. So the arc length of this sector is 6π.

In fact, this rule applies even more generally to circles. If, instead of cutting the circle in half, you had cut it into quarters, each piece of the circle would have 1/4 the area of the entire circle and 1/4 the circumference:

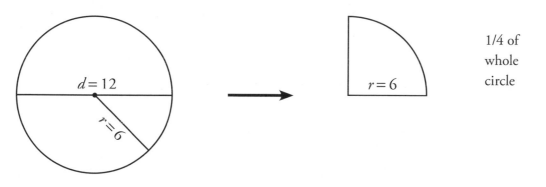

1/4 of whole circle

Now, on the GRE, you're unlikely to be told that you have one-quarter of a circle. There is one more basic element of circles that becomes relevant when you are dealing with sectors, and that is the **central angle**. The central angle of a sector is the degree measure between the two radii. Take a look at the quarter circle. There are 360° in a full circle. What is the degree measure of the angle between the two radii? The same thing that happens to area and circumference happens to the central angle. It is now 1/4 of 360°, which is 90°:

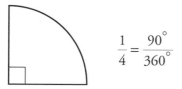

$$\frac{1}{4} = \frac{90^\circ}{360^\circ}$$

How can you use the central angle to determine sector area and arc length? For the next example, you will still use the circle with area 36π, but now the sector will have a central angle of 60°:

You need to figure out what fractional amount of the circle remains if the central angle is 60°. If 360° is the whole amount, and 60° is the part, then 60/360 is the fraction you're looking for, and 60/360 reduces to 1/6.

That means a sector with a central angle of 60° is 1/6 of the entire circle. If that's the case, then the sector area is $\frac{1}{6} \times$ (Area of circle) and arc length is $\frac{1}{6} \times$ (Circumference of circle). So:

$$\text{Sector Area} = \frac{1}{6} \times (36\pi) = 6\pi$$

$$\text{Arc Length} = \frac{1}{6} \times (12\pi) = 2\pi$$

$$\frac{1}{6} = \frac{60^{\circ}}{360^{\circ}} = \frac{\text{Sector Area}}{\text{Circle Area}} = \frac{\text{Arc Length}}{\text{Circumference}}$$

In this last example, you used the central angle to find what fractional amount of the circle the sector was. But any of the three properties of a sector (central angle, arc length, and area) could be used if you know the radius.

Here's an example:

A sector has a radius of 9 and an area of 27π. What is the central angle of the sector?

You still need to determine what fractional amount of the circle the sector is. This time, however, you have to use the area to figure that out. You know the area of the sector, so if you can figure out the area of the whole circle, you can figure out what fractional amount the sector is.

You know the radius is 9, so you can calculate the area of the whole circle. Area = πr^2, so Area = $\pi(9)^2 = 81\pi$. Because $\frac{27\pi}{81\pi} = \frac{1}{3}$, the sector is 1/3 of the circle. The full circle has a central angle of 360°, so the central angle of the sector is 1/3 × 360 = 120°:

$$\frac{1}{3} = \frac{120^{\circ}}{360^{\circ}} = \frac{27\pi \ (\text{sector area})}{81\pi \ (\text{circle area})}$$

Now recap what you know about sectors. Every question about sectors involves determining what fraction of the circle the sector is. That means that every question about sectors will provide you with enough information to calculate one of the following fractions:

$$\frac{\text{central angle}}{360} = \frac{\text{sector area}}{\text{circle area}} = \frac{\text{arc length}}{\text{circumference}}$$

Once you know any of those fractions, you know them all, and, if you know any specific value, you can find the value of any piece of the sector or the original circle.

Check Your Skills

4. A sector has a central angle of 270° and a radius of 2. What is the area of the sector?
5. A sector has an arc length of 4π and a radius of 3. What is the central angle of the sector?
6. A sector has an area of 40π and a radius of 10. What is the arc length of the sector?

Answers can be found on page 113.

Inscribed vs. Central Angles

Thus far, in dealing with arcs and sectors, the concept of a **central angle** has been noted. A central angle is defined as an angle whose vertex lies at the center point of a circle. As you have seen, a central angle defines both an arc and a sector of a circle.

Another type of angle is termed an **inscribed angle**. An inscribed angle has its vertex *on the circle itself* (rather than on the *center* of the circle). The following diagrams illustrate the difference between a central angle and an inscribed angle:

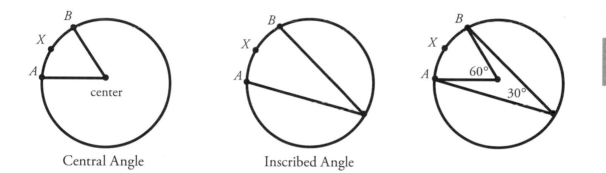

Central Angle   Inscribed Angle

Notice that, in the circle at the far right, there is a central angle and an inscribed angle, both of which intercept arc *AXB*. It is the central angle that defines the arc. That is, the arc is 60° (or one-sixth of the complete 360° circle). **An inscribed angle is equal to half of the arc it intercepts**, in degrees. In this case, the inscribed angle is 30°, which is half of 60°.

Inscribed Triangles

Related to this idea of an inscribed angle is that of an **inscribed triangle**. A triangle is said to be inscribed in a circle if all of the vertices of the triangle are points on the circle.

The figure on the next page shows a special case of the rule mentioned above (that an inscribed angle is equal to half of the arc it intercepts, in degrees). In this case, the right angle (90°) lies opposite a semicircle, which is an arc that measures 180°.

The important rule to remember is: **If one of the sides of an inscribed triangle is a *diameter* of the circle, then the triangle *must* be a right triangle.** Conversely, any right triangle inscribed in a circle must have the diameter of the circle as one of its sides (thereby splitting the circle in half).

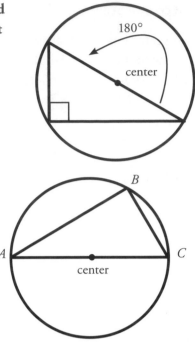

In the inscribed triangle to the right, triangle *ABC* must be a right triangle, since *AC* is a diameter of the circle.

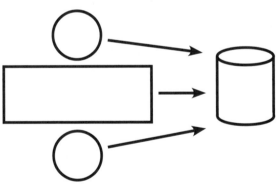

Cylinders and Surface Area

Two circles and a rectangle combine to form a three-dimensional shape called a right circular cylinder (referred to from now on simply as a **cylinder**). The top and bottom of the cylinder are circles, while the middle of the cylinder is formed from a rolled-up rectangle, as shown in the diagram.

In order to determine the surface area of a cylinder, sum the areas of the three surfaces: The area of each circle is πr^2, while the area of the rectangle is length × width.

Looking at the figure on the right, you can see that the length of the rectangle is equal to the circumference of the circle ($2\pi r$), and the width of the rectangle is equal to the height of the cylinder (h). Therefore, the area of the rectangle is $2\pi r \times h$. To find the total surface area (SA) of a cylinder, add the area of the circular top and bottom, as well as the area of the rectangle that wraps around the outside. To review:

$$\boxed{SA = 2 \text{ circles} + \text{rectangle} = 2(\pi r^2) + 2\pi rh}$$

The only information you need to find the surface area of a cylinder is 1) the radius of the cylinder, and 2) the height of the cylinder.

Cylinders and Volume

The volume of a cylinder measures how much "stuff" it can hold inside. In order to find the volume of a cylinder, use the following formula, where V is the volume, r is the radius of the cylinder, and h is the height of the cylinder:

$$V = \pi r^2 h$$

As with finding the surface area, determining the volume of a cylinder requires two pieces of information: 1) the radius of the cylinder, and 2) the height of the cylinder.

One way to remember this formula is to think of a cylinder as a stack of circles, each with an area of πr^2. Just multiply $\pi r^2 \times$ the height (h) of the shape to find the area.

The figures below show that two cylinders can have the same volume but different shapes (and, therefore, each would fit differently inside a larger object):

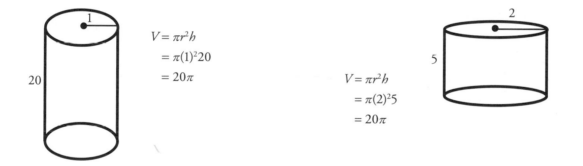

5

Check Your Skills Answer Key

1. **49π:** The formula for area is $A = \pi r^2$. The radius is 7, so the area is $\pi(7)^2 = 49\pi$.

2. **17:** Circumference of a circle is either $C = 2\pi r$ or $C = \pi d$. The question asks for the diameter, so use the latter formula: $17\pi = \pi d$. Divide by π, and you get $17 = d$.

3. **10π:** The link between area and circumference of a circle is that they are both defined in terms of the radius. Area of a circle is $A = \pi r^2$, so you can use the area of the circle to find the radius: $25\pi = \pi r^2$, so $r = 5$. If the radius equals 5, then the circumference is $C = 2\pi(5)$, which equals 10π.

4. **3π:** If the central angle of the sector is 270°, then it is 3/4 of the full circle, because $\dfrac{270°}{360°} = \dfrac{3}{4}$. If the radius is 2, then the area of the full circle is $\pi(2)^2$, which equals 4π. If the area of the full circle is 4π, then the area of the sector will be $3/4 \times 4\pi$, which equals 3π.

5. **240°:** To find the central angle, you first need to figure out what fraction of the circle the sector is. You can do that by finding the circumference of the full circle. The radius is 3, so the circumference of the circle is $2\pi(3) = 6\pi$. That means the sector is 2/3 of the circle, because $\dfrac{4\pi}{6\pi} = \dfrac{2}{3}$. That means the central angle of the sector is 2/3 × 360°, which equals 240°.

6. **8π:** Begin by finding the area of the whole circle. The radius of the circle is 10, so the area is $\pi(10)^2$, which equals 100π. That means the sector is 2/5 of the circle, because $\dfrac{40\pi}{100\pi} = \dfrac{4}{10} = \dfrac{2}{5}$. You can find the circumference of the whole circle using $C = 2\pi r = 2\pi(10) = 20\pi$. You can find the arc length of the sector by taking 2/5 × 20π = 8π. The arc length of the sector is 8π.

5

Problem Set

(Note: Figures are not drawn to scale.)

1. Triangle *ABC* is inscribed in a circle, such that *AC* is a diameter of the circle (see figure). What is the circumference of the circle?

2. A cylinder has a surface area of 360π and height of 3. What is the diameter of the cylinder's circular base?

3. Randy can run π meters every 2 seconds. If the circular track has a radius of 75 meters, how many minutes does it take Randy to run twice around the track?

4. Randy then moves on to the Jumbo Track, which has a radius of 200 meters (as compared to the first track, with a radius of 75 meters). Ordinarily, Randy runs 8 laps on the normal track. How many laps on the Jumbo Track would Randy have to run in order to run the same distance?

5. A circular lawn with a radius of 5 meters is surrounded by a circular walkway that is 4 meters wide (see figure). What is the area of the walkway?

6. A cylindrical water tank has a diameter of 14 meters and a height of 20 meters. A water truck can fill π cubic meters of the tank every minute. How long in hours and minutes will it take the water truck to fill the water tank from empty to half full?

7. *AC* and *DE* are both diameters of the circle in the figure to the right. If the area of the circle is 180 units², what is the total area of the shaded sectors?

8. Jane has to paint a cylindrical column that is 14 feet high and that has a circular base with a radius of 3 feet. If one bucket of paint will cover 10π square feet, how many whole buckets does Jane need to buy in order to paint the column, including the top and bottom?

9. A circular flower bed takes up half the area of a square lawn. If an edge of the lawn is 200 feet long, what is the radius of the flower bed? (Express the answer in terms of π.)

10. If angle *ACB* is 40 degrees (see figure), and the area of the circle is 81π, how long is arc *AXB*?

11. Triangle *ABD* is inscribed in a circle, such that *AD* is a diameter of the circle and angle *BAD* is 45° (see figure). If the area of triangle *ABD* is 72 square units, how much larger is the area of the circle than the area of triangle *ABD*?

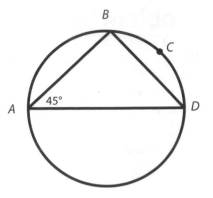

12. Triangle *ABD* is inscribed in a circle, such that *AD* is a diameter of the circle. (Refer to the same figure as for problem #11.) If the area of triangle *ABD* is 84.5 square units, what is the length of arc *BCD*?

13.

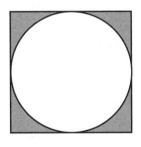

A is the center of the circle above.

Quantity A	**Quantity B**
The perimeter of triangle *ABC*	The perimeter of the shaded region

14.

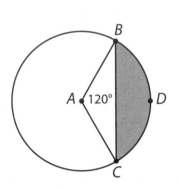

In the figure above, a circle with area π is inscribed in a square.

Quantity A	**Quantity B**
The combined area of the shaded regions	1

15.

Quantity A	**Quantity B**
The combined area of four circles, each with radius 1	The area of a circle with radius 2

Solutions

1. **17π:** If AC is a diameter of the circle, then inscribed triangle ABC is a right triangle, with AC as the hypotenuse. Therefore, you can apply the Pythagorean theorem to find the length of AC:

$$8^2 + 15^2 = (AC)^2$$
$$64 + 225 = (AC)^2$$
$$(AC)^2 = 289$$
$$(AC) = 17$$

You might recognize the common 8–15–17 right triangle.

AC is the diameter of the circle, so $d = 17$. The circumference of the circle is πd, or 17π.

2. **24:** The surface area of a cylinder is the area of the circular top and bottom, plus the area of its wrapped-around rectangular third face. You can express this in formula form as:

$$SA = 2(\pi r^2) + 2\pi rh$$

Substitute the known values into this formula to find the radius of the circular base:

$$360\pi = 2(\pi r^2) + 2\pi r(3)$$
$$360\pi = 2\pi r^2 + 6\pi r$$
$$0 = 2\pi r^2 + 6\pi r - 360\pi$$
$$0 = r^2 + 3r - 180 \qquad \text{Divide by } 2\pi.$$
$$0 = (r + 15)(r - 12)$$

$$r + 15 = 0 \qquad \text{OR} \qquad r - 12 = 0$$
$$r = \{-15, 12\}$$

Use only the positive value of r, which is 12. If $r = 12$, the diameter of the cylinder's circular base is 24.

3. **10 minutes:** The distance around the track is the circumference of the circle:

$$C = 2\pi r$$
$$C = 150\pi$$

Running twice around the circle would equal a distance of 300π meters. If Randy can run π meters every 2 seconds, he runs 30π meters every minute. Therefore, it will take him 10 minutes to run around the circular track twice.

4. **3 laps:** 8 laps on the normal track is a distance of $1{,}200\pi$ meters. (Recall from problem #3 that the circumference of the normal track is 150π meters.) If the Jumbo Track has a radius of 200 meters, its circumference is 400π meters. It will take 3 laps around this track to travel $1{,}200\pi$ meters.

5. **$56\pi\,\text{m}^2$:** The area of the walkway is the area of the entire image (walkway + lawn) minus the area of the lawn. To find the area of each circle, use the formula:

Large circle:	$A = \pi r^2 = \pi(9)^2 = 81\pi$	
Small circle:	$A = \pi r^2 = \pi(5)^2 = 25\pi$	$81\pi - 25\pi = 56\pi\,\text{m}^2$

6. **8 hours and 10 minutes:** First find the volume of the cylindrical tank:

$$V = \pi r^2 \times h$$
$$= \pi(7)^2 \times 20$$
$$= 980\pi$$

If the water truck can fill π cubic meters of the tank every minute, it will take 980 minutes to fill the tank completely; therefore, it will take $980 \div 2 = 490$ minutes to fill the tank halfway. This is equal to 8 hours and 10 minutes.

7. **40 units²:** The two central angles of the shaded sectors include a total of 80°. Simplify the fraction to find out what fraction of the circle this represents:

$$\frac{80}{360} = \frac{2}{9} \qquad \frac{2}{9} \text{ of 180 units}^2 \text{ is 40 units}^2.$$

8. **11 buckets:** The surface area of a cylinder is the area of the circular top and bottom, plus the area of its wrapped-around rectangular third face:

Top & Bottom:	$A = \pi r^2 = 9\pi$ (each)	
Rectangle:	$A = 2\pi r \times h = 84\pi$	

The total surface area, then, is $9\pi + 9\pi + 84\pi = 102\pi\,\text{ft}^2$. If one bucket of paint will cover $10\pi\,\text{ft}^2$, then Jane will need 10.2 buckets to paint the entire column. Since paint stores do not sell fractional buckets, she will need to purchase 11 buckets.

9. $\sqrt{\dfrac{20,000}{\pi}}$ **ft:** The area of the lawn is $(200)^2 = 40,000\,\text{ft}^2$.

Therefore, the area of the flower bed is $40,000 \div 2 = 20,000\,\text{ft}^2$.

$$A = \pi r^2 = 20,000 \qquad \text{The radius of the flower bed is equal to } \sqrt{\frac{20,000}{\pi}}.$$

10. **4π:** If the area of the circle is 81π, then the radius of the circle is 9 (from $A = \pi r^2$). Therefore, the total circumference of the circle is 18π (from $C = 2\pi r$). Angle ACB, an inscribed angle of 40°, corresponds to a central angle of 80°. Thus, arc AXB is equal to $80/360 = 2/9$ of the total circumference:

$$\frac{2}{9}(18\pi) = 4\pi$$

MANHATTAN
PREP

11. **$72\pi - 72$ square units:** If AD is a diameter of the circle, then angle ABD is a right angle. Therefore, triangle ABD is a 45–45–90 triangle, and the base and height are equal. Assign the variable x to represent both the base and height (i.e., the legs of a right triangle):

$$A = \frac{bh}{2}$$
$$\frac{x^2}{2} = 72$$
$$x^2 = 144$$
$$x = 12$$

To check, the base and height of the triangle are equal to 12, and so the area of the triangle is $\frac{12 \times 12}{2} = 72$.

The hypotenuse of the triangle, which is also the diameter of the circle, is equal to $12\sqrt{2}$. Therefore, the radius is equal to $6\sqrt{2}$ and the area of the circle is $\pi r^2 = \pi(6\sqrt{2})^2 = 72\pi$. The area of the circle is $72\pi - 72$ square units larger than the area of triangle ABD.

12. $\dfrac{13\sqrt{2} \times \pi}{4}$ **units:** You know that the area of triangle ABD is 84.5 square units, so you can use the same logic as in the previous problem to establish the base and height of the triangle:

$$A = \frac{bh}{2}$$
$$\frac{x^2}{2} = 84.5$$
$$x^2 = 169$$
$$x = 13$$

The base and height of the triangle are equal to 13. Therefore, the hypotenuse, which is also the diameter of the circle, is equal to $13\sqrt{2}$, and the circumference ($C = \pi d$) is equal to $13\sqrt{2} \times \pi$. The labeled 45° angle, which is the inscribed angle for arc BCD corresponds to a central angle of 90°. Thus, arc $BCD = 90/360 = 1/4$ of the total circumference:

$$\frac{1}{4} \text{ of } 13\sqrt{2} \times \pi \text{ is } \frac{13\sqrt{2} \times \pi}{4}$$

13. **(B):** Since the two perimeters share the line BC, you can recast this question:

Quantity A	**Quantity B**
The combined length of two radii (AB and AC)	The length of arc BDC

The easiest thing to do in this situation is use numbers. Assume the radius of the circle is 2. If the radius is 2, then you can rewrite Quantity A:

Quantity A	**Quantity B**
The combined length of two radii (AB and AC) = **4**	The length of arc BDC

Now you need to figure out the length of arc *BDC* if the radius is 2. You can set up a proportion, because the ratio of central angle to 360° will be the same as the ratio of the arc length to the circumference:

$$\frac{\text{Arc Length}}{\text{Circumference}} = \frac{120°}{360°} = \frac{1}{3}$$

Circumference is $2\pi r$, so:

$$C = 2\pi(2) = 4\pi$$

Rewrite the proportion:

$$\frac{\text{Arc Length}}{4\pi} = \frac{1}{3}$$

$$\text{Arc Length} = \frac{4\pi}{3}$$

Rewrite Quantity B:

Quantity A	**Quantity B**
4	The length of arc $BDC = \dfrac{4\pi}{3}$

Compare 4 to $4\pi/3$. π is greater than 3, so $\dfrac{4\pi}{3}$ is slightly greater than 4.

14. **(B):** Use the area of the circle to determine the area of the square, then subtract the area of the circle from the area of the square to determine the shaded region. The formula for area of a circle is $A = \pi r^2$. If you substitute the area of this circle for A, you can determine the radius:

$$\pi = \pi r^2$$
$$1 = r^2$$
$$1 = r$$

Since the radius of the circle is 1, the diameter of the circle is 2, as is each side of the square. A square with sides of 2 has an area of 4. Rewrite Quantity A:

Quantity A	**Quantity B**
The combined area of the shaded regions = $\text{Area}_{\text{Square}} - \text{Area}_{\text{Circle}} = \mathbf{4 - \pi}$	1

Since π is greater than 3, $4 - \pi$ is less than 1. Therefore, **Quantity B is greater**.

15. **(C):** First, evaluate Quantity A. Plug in 1 for *r* in the formula for the area of a circle:

$A = \pi r^2$
$A = \pi(1)^2$
$A = \pi$

Each circle has an area of π, and the four circles have a total area of 4π.

Quantity A	**Quantity B**
The combined area of four circles, each with radius 1 = **4π**	The area of a circle with radius 2

For Quantity B, plug in 2 for *r* in the formula for the area of a circle:

$A = \pi r^2$
$A = \pi(2)^2$
$A = 4\pi$

Quantity A	**Quantity B**
4π	The area of a circle with radius 2 = **4π**

Therefore, **the two quantities are equal**.

5

Chapter 6

of

Geometry

Lines & Angles

In This Chapter...

Chapter 6
Lines & Angles

A straight line is 180°. Think of a line as half of a circle:

Parallel lines are lines that lie in a plane and never intersect. No matter how far you extend the lines, they never meet. Two parallel lines are shown below:

Perpendicular lines are lines that intersect at a 90° angle. Two perpendicular lines are shown below:

There are two major line-angle relationships that you must know for the GRE:

1. The angles formed by any intersecting lines.
2. The angles formed by parallel lines cut by a transversal.

Intersecting Lines

Intersecting lines have three important properties.

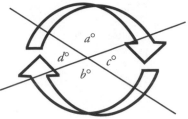

First, the interior angles formed by intersecting lines form a circle, so the sum of these angles is 360°. In the diagram shown on the right, $a + b + c + d = 360$.

Second, interior angles that combine to form a line sum to 180°. These are termed **supplementary angles**. Thus, in the same diagram shown, $a + d = 180$, because angles a and d form a line together. Other supplementary angles are $b + c = 180$, $a + c = 180$, and $d + b = 180$.

Third, angles found opposite each other where these two lines intersect are equal. These are called **vertical angles**. Thus, in the diagram above, $a = b$, because these angles are opposite one another and are formed from the same two lines. Additionally, $c = d$ for the same reason.

Note that these rules apply to more than two lines that intersect at a point, as shown to the right. In this diagram, $a + b + c + d + e + f = 360$, because these angles combine to form a circle. In addition, $a + b + c = 180$, because these three angles combine to form a line. Finally, $a = d$, $b = e$, and $c = f$, because they are pairs of vertical angles.

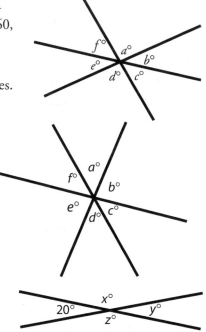

Check Your Skills

1. If $b + f = 150$, what is d?

2. What is $x - y$?

Answers can be found on page 129.

Exterior Angles of a Triangle

An **exterior angle** of a triangle is equal in measure to the sum of the two non-adjacent (opposite) **interior angles** of the triangle. For example:

$a + b + c = 180$ (sum of angles in a triangle)
$b + x = 180$ (supplementary angles)
Therefore, $x = a + c$.

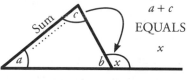

This property is frequently tested on the GRE! In particular, look for exterior angles within more complicated diagrams. You might even redraw the diagram with certain lines removed to isolate the triangle and exterior angle you need:

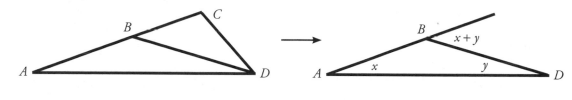

Check Your Skills

3. If $c + d = 200$, what is $a + b$?

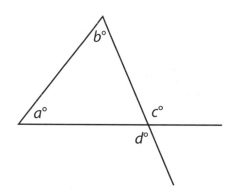

The answer can be found on page 129.

6

Parallel Lines Cut By a Transversal

The GRE makes frequent use of diagrams that include parallel lines cut by a **transversal**.

Notice that there are eight angles formed by this construction, but there are only *two* different angle measures (a and b). All the **acute** angles (less than 90°) in this diagram are equal. Likewise, all the **obtuse** angles (more than 90° but less than 180°) are equal. The acute angles are supplementary to the obtuse angles. Thus, $a + b = 180°$.

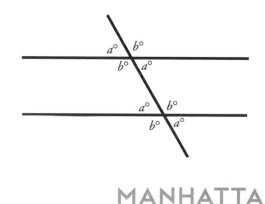

When you see a third line intersecting two lines that you know to be parallel, fill in all the *a* (acute) and *b* (obtuse) angles, just as in the diagram above.

Sometimes the GRE disguises the parallel lines and the transversal so that they are not readily apparent, as in the diagram pictured to the right.

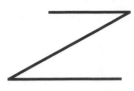

In these disguised cases, it is a good idea to extend the lines so that you can easily see the parallel lines and the transversal. Just remember always to be on the lookout for parallel lines. When you see them, extend lines and label the acute and obtuse angles.

You might also mark the parallel lines with arrows.

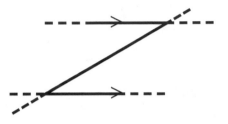

Check Your Skills

Refer to the following diagram for questions #4–5.

(lines *p* and *q* are parallel)

4. If *g* = 120, what is *a*?
5. If *g* = 120, what is *a* + *b* + *c*?

Answers can be found on page 129.

Check Your Skills Answer Key

1. **30°:** Because they are vertical angles, angle a is equal to angle d.

Because they add to form a straight line: $a + b + f = 180$.

Substitute d for a to yield: $(d) + b + f = 180$. Substitute 150 for $b + f$ to yield: $d + (150) = 180$. Thus, $d = 180 - 150 = 30$.

2. **140°:** Because $x°$ and $20°$ are supplementary, $x = 180 - 20 = 160$. Because $y°$ and $20°$ are vertical, $y = 20$. So $x - y = 160 - 20 = 140$.

3. **100°:** Since c and d are vertical angles, they are equal. Since they sum to 200, each must be 100. $a + b = c$, because c is an exterior angle of the triangle shown, and a and b are the two non-adjacent interior angles. $a + b = c = 100$.

4. **120°:** In a system of parallel lines cut by a transversal, opposite exterior angles (like a and g) are equal. $g = a = 120$.

5. **300°:** From question 4, you know that $a = 120$. Since $a = 120$, its supplementary angle $d = 180 - 120 = 60$. Since $a + b + c + d = 360$, and $d = 60$, then $a + b + c = 300$.

6

Problem Set (Note: Figures are not drawn to scale.)

Problems #1–4 refer to the diagram on the right, where line *AB* is parallel to line *CD*. Note: Figures are not drawn to scale.

1. If $x - y = 10$, what is x?

2. If the ratio of x to y is $3 : 2$, what is y?

3. If $x + (x + y) = 320$, what is x?

4. If $\dfrac{x}{x-y} = 2$, what is x?

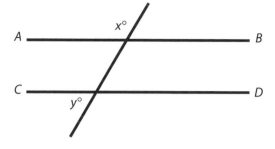

Problems #5–8 refer to the diagram on the right.

5. If $a = 95$, what is $b + d - e$?

6. If $c + f = 70$, and $d = 80$, what is b?

7. If a and b are **complementary angles** (they sum to 90°), name three other pairs of complementary angles.

8. If $e = 45$, what is the sum of all the other angles?

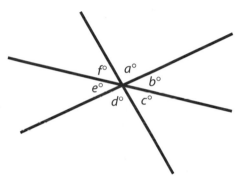

Problems #9–12 refer to the diagram on the right, where line *XY* is parallel to line *QU*.

9. If $a + e = 150$, find f.

10. If $a = y$, $g - 3y + 20$, and $f = 2x$, find x.

11. If $g = 11y$, $a = 4x - y$, and $d = 5y + 2x - 20$, find h.

12. If $b = 4x$, $e = x + 2y$, and $d = 3y + 8$, find h.

Problems #13–15 refer to the diagram to the right.

13. If $c + f = 140$, find k.

14. If $f = 90$, what is $a + k$?

15. If $f + k = 150$, find b.

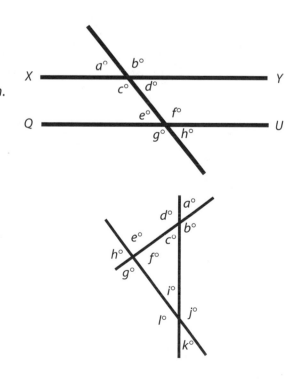

16.

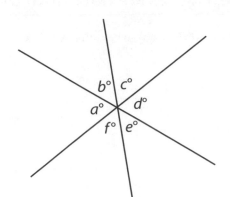

Quantity A	**Quantity B**
$a + f + b$	$c + d + e$

17.

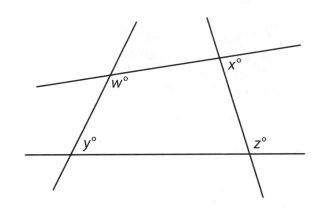

Quantity A	**Quantity B**
$w + y$	$x + z$

18.

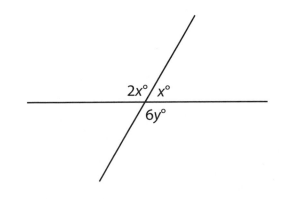

Quantity A	**Quantity B**
y	10

MANHATTAN
PREP

Solutions

1. 95°: You know that $x + y = 180$, since any acute angle formed by a transversal that cuts across two parallel lines is supplementary to any obtuse angle formed in the same figure. Use the information given to set up a system of two equations with two variables:

$$\begin{aligned} x + y &= 180 \\ x - y &= 10 \\ \hline 2x &= 190 \\ x &= 95 \end{aligned}$$

2. 72°: Set up a ratio, using the unknown multiplier, a:

Set $x = 3a$ and $y = 2a$, so $\dfrac{x}{y} = \dfrac{3a}{2a}$

$180 = x + y = 3a + 2a = 5a$

$180 = 5a$

$a = 36$

$y = 2a = 2(36) = 72$

3. 140°: Use the fact that $x + y = 180$ to set up a system of two equations with two variables:

$$x + y = 180 \quad \rightarrow \quad \begin{aligned} -x - y &= -180 \\ +\quad 2x + y &= 320 \\ \hline x &= 140 \end{aligned}$$

4. 120°: First, simplify the given equation. Then, use the fact that $x + y = 180$ to set up a system of two equations with two variables.

$$\frac{x}{(x - y)} = 2 \qquad\qquad\qquad 0 = x - 2y$$
$$x = 2(x - y) \qquad\qquad \underline{-(180 = x + y)}$$
$$x = 2x - 2y \qquad\qquad -180 = -3y$$
$$0 = x - 2y \qquad\qquad\quad 60 = y \quad \rightarrow \quad \text{Therefore, } x = 120$$

5. 95°: Because a and d are vertical angles, they have the same measure: $a = d = 95$. Likewise, since b and e are vertical angles, they have the same measure: $b = e$. Therefore, $b + d - e = d = 95$.

6. 65°: Because c and f are vertical angles, they have the same measure: $c + f = 70$, so $c = f = 35$. Notice that b, c, and d form a straight line: $b + c + d = 180$. Substitute the known values of c and d into this equation:

$$\begin{aligned} b + 35 + 80 &= 180 \\ b + 115 &= 180 \\ b &= 65 \end{aligned}$$

7. **b and d, a and e, & d and e:** If a is complementary to b, then d (which is equal to a, since they are vertical angles), is also complementary to b. Likewise, if a is complementary to b, then a is also complementary to e (which is equal to b, since they are vertical angles). Finally, d and e must be complementary, since $d = a$ and $e = b$. You do not need to know the term "complementary," but you should be able to work with the concept (two angles adding up to 90°).

8. **315°:** If $e = 45$, then the sum of all the other angles is $360 - 45 = 315$.

9. **105°:** You are told that $a + e = 150$. Since they are both acute angles formed by a transversal cutting across two parallel lines, they are also equal. Therefore, $a = e = 75$. Any acute angle in this diagram is supplementary to any obtuse angle, so $75 + f = 180$, and $f = 105$.

10. **70°:** You know that angles a and g are supplementary; their measures sum to 180. Therefore:

$$y + 3y + 20 = 180$$
$$4y = 160$$
$$y = 40$$

Angle f is equal to angle g, so its measure is also $3y + 20$. The measure of angle $f = g = 3(40) + 20 = 140$. If $f = 2x$, then $140 = 2x$ and, therefore $x = 70$.

11. **70°:** You are given the measure of one acute angle (a) and one obtuse angle (g). Since any acute angle in this diagram is supplementary to any obtuse angle, then $11y + 4x - y = 180$, or $4x + 10y = 180$. Since angle d is equal to angle a, then $5y + 2x - 20 = 4x - y$, or $2x - 6y = -20$. You can set up a system of two equations with two variables:

$$2x - 6y = -20 \quad \rightarrow \quad \begin{aligned} -4x + 12y &= 40 \\ 4x + 10y &= 180 \\ \hline 22y &= 220 \\ y = 10; \; x &= 20 \end{aligned}$$

Since h is one of the acute angles, h has the same measure as a: $4x - y = 4(20) - 10 = 70$.

12. **68°:** Because b and d are supplementary, $4x + 3y + 8 = 180$ or $4x + 3y = 172$. Since d and e are equal, $3y + 8 = x + 2y$ or $x - y = 8$. You can set up a system of two equations with two variables:

$$x - y = 8 \quad \rightarrow \quad \begin{aligned} 4x + 3y &= 172 \\ 3x - 3y &= 24 \\ \hline 7x &= 196 \\ x &= 28; \; y = 20 \end{aligned}$$

Since h is equal to e, $h = x + 2y$, or $28 + 2(20) + 8 = 68$.

13. **40°:** If $c + f = 140$, then $i = 40$, because there are 180° in a triangle. Since k is vertical to i, k is also equal to 40. Alternatively, if $c + f = 140$, then $l = 140$, since l is an exterior angle of the triangle and is therefore equal to the sum of the two remote interior angles. Since k is supplementary to l, $k = 180 - 140 = 40$.

14. **90°:** If $f = 90$, then the other two angles in the triangle, c and i, sum to 90. Since a and k are vertical angles to c and i, they sum to 90 as well.

15. **150°:** Angle k is vertical to angle i. So if $f + k = 150$, then $f + i = 150$. Angle b, an exterior angle of the triangle, must be equal to the sum of the two remote interior angles, f and i. Therefore, $b = 150$.

16. **(C):** You can substitute each of the values in Quantity A for a corresponding value in Quantity B: $a = d$, $c = f$, and $b = e$, in each case because the equal angles are vertical angles. Rewrite Quantity A:

Quantity A   **Quantity B**

$a + f + b = (d) + (c) + (e)$ $c + d + e$

Therefore, **the two quantities are equal**.

17. **(C):** To see why the sums in the two quantities are equal, label the remaining two interior angles of the quadrilateral according to the rules for supplementary angles:

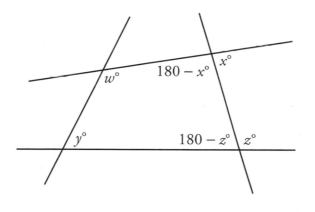

Quantity A   **Quantity B**

$w + y$ $x + z$

There are several relationships that can be described based on the diagram. For instance, you know the sum of the four internal angles of the quadrilateral is 360:

$$w + y + (180 - x) + (180 - z) = 360$$
$$w + y - x - z = 0$$
$$w + y = x + z$$

Therefore, the **two quantities are equal**.

18. **(A):** First solve for x. The two angles x and $2x$ are supplementary:

$$x + 2x = 180$$
$$3x = 180$$
$$x = 60$$

Next note that $2x = 6y$, because $2x$ and $6y$ are vertical angles. Plug in 60 for x and solve for y:

$$2(60) = 6y$$
$$120 = 6y$$
$$20 = y$$

Quantity A	**Quantity B**
$y = \mathbf{20}$	10

Therefore, **Quantity A is greater.**

6

Chapter 7
of Geometry

The Coordinate Plane

In This Chapter...

Chapter 7

The Coordinate Plane

Before examining the coordinate plane, you should review the number line:

The Number Line

The number line is a ruler or measuring stick that goes as far as you want in both directions. With the number line, you can say where something is positioned with a single number. In other words, you can link a position with a number:

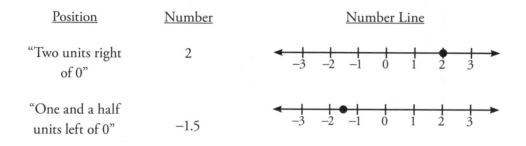

Position	Number	Number Line
"Two units right of 0"	2	
"One and a half units left of 0"	−1.5	

You use both positive and negative numbers, because you can indicate positions both left and right of 0.

You might be wondering, "The position of what?" The answer is, a **point**, which is just a dot. When you are dealing with the number line, a point and a number mean the same thing:

If you show me where the point is on the number line, I can tell you the number.

The point is at −2.

If you tell me the number, I can show you where the point is on the number line.

The point is at 0.

This works even if you only have partial information about your point. If told *something* about where the point is, you can say *something* about the number, and vice versa.

For instance, if told that the number is positive, then you know that the point lies somewhere to the right of 0 on the number line. Even though you don't know the exact location of the point, you do know a range of potential values:

The number is positive.
In other words, the number is greater than (>) 0.

Therefore,

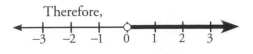

The open circle means 0 is not included.

This also works in reverse. If you see a range of potential positions on a number line, you can tell what that range is for the number:

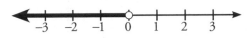

Therefore, the number is less than (<) 0.

Now to make things more complicated. What if you want to be able to locate a point that's not on a straight line, but on a page?

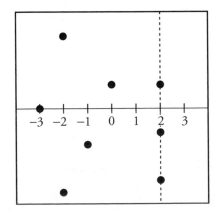

The point you want.

Now one number line won't be enough to tell you where the point is.

7

Begin by inserting your number line into the picture. This will help you determine how far to the right or left of 0 your point is:

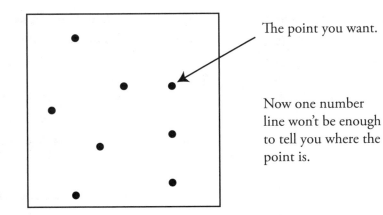

The point is 2 units to the right of 0.

But all three points that touch the dotted line are 2 units to the right of 0. You don't have enough information to determine the unique location of the point.

In order to know the location of your point, you also need to know how far up or down the dotted line you need to go. To determine how far up or down you need to go, you're going to need another number line. This number line, however, is going to be vertical. Using this vertical number line, you will be able to measure how far above or below 0 a point is:

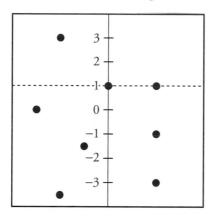

The point is 1 unit above 0.

Notice that this number line by itself also does not provide enough information to determine the unique location of the point.

But, if you combine the information from the two number lines, you can determine both how far left or right *and* how far up or down the point is:

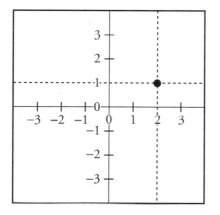

The point is 2 units to the right of 0.

AND

The point is 1 unit above 0.

Now you have a unique description of the point's position. There is only one point on the page that is BOTH 2 units to the right of 0 AND 1 unit above 0. So, on a page, you need two numbers to indicate position.

Just as with the number line, information can travel in either direction. If you know the two numbers that give the location, you can place that point on the page:

The point is 3 units to the left of 0.

AND

The point is 2 units below 0.

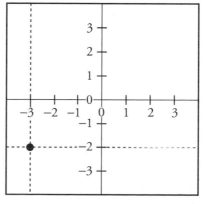

If, on the other hand, you see a point on the page, you can identify its location and determine the two numbers:

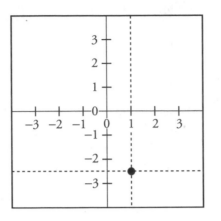

The point is 1 unit to the right of 0.

AND

The point is 2.5 units below 0.

Now that you have two pieces of information for each point, you need to keep straight which number is which. In other words, you need to know which number gives the left-right position and which number gives the up-down position.

To represent the difference, use some technical terms:

The **x-coordinate** is the left-right number:

> Numbers to the right of 0 are positive.
> Numbers to the left of 0 are negative.

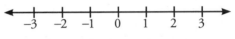

This number line is the **x-axis**.

The **y-coordinate** is the up-down number:

> Numbers above 0 are positive.
> Numbers below 0 are negative.

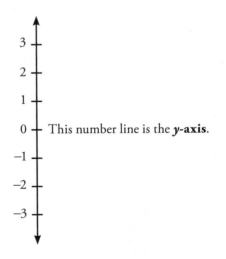

This number line is the **y-axis**.

Now, when describing the location of a point, you can use the technical terms:

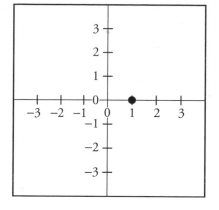

The *x*-coordinate of the point is 1 and the *y*-coordinate of the point is 0.

You can condense this and say that, for this point, *x* = 1 and *y* = 0. In fact, you can go even further. You can say that the point is at (1, 0). This shorthand always has the same basic layout. The first number in the parentheses is the *x*-coordinate, and the second number is the *y*-coordinate. One easy way to remember this is that *x* comes before *y* in the alphabet. For example:

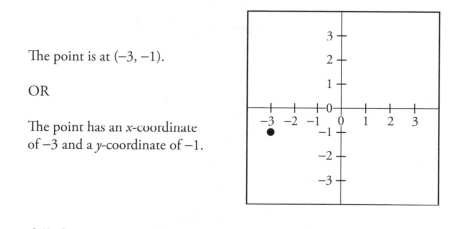

The point is at (−3, −1).

OR

The point has an *x*-coordinate of −3 and a *y*-coordinate of −1.

Now you have a fully functioning **coordinate plane**: an *x*-axis and a *y*-axis drawn on a page. The coordinate plane allows you to determine the unique position of any point on a **plane** (essentially, a really big and flat sheet of paper).

And in case you were ever curious about what one dimensional and two dimensional mean, now you know. A line is one dimensional, because you only need *one* number to identify a point's location. A plane is two-dimensional because you need *two* numbers to identify a point's location.

<u>Check Your Skills</u>

1. Draw a coordinate plane and plot the following points:

      1. (3, 1)   2. (−2, 3.5)   3. (0, −4.5)   4. (1, 0)

2. Which point on the coordinate plane below is indicated by the following coordinates?

      1. (2, −1)   2. (−1.5, −3)   3. (−1, 2)   4. (3, 2)   5. (2, 3)

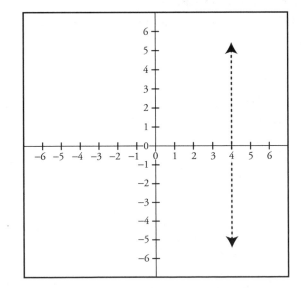

Answers can be found on page 163.

Knowing Just One Coordinate

As you've just seen, you need to know both the *x*-coordinate and the *y*-coordinate to plot a point exactly on the coordinate plane. If you only know one coordinate, you can't tell precisely where the point is, but you can narrow down the possibilities.

Consider this situation. Say that this is all you know: the point is 4 units to the right of 0:

As you saw earlier, any point along the vertical dotted line is 4 units to the right of 0. In other words, every point on the dotted line has an x-coordinate of 4. You could shorten that and say $x = 4$. You don't know anything about the y-coordinate, which could be any number. All the points along the dotted line have different y-coordinates but the same x-coordinate, which equals 4.

So, if you know that $x = 4$, then your point can be anywhere along a vertical line that crosses the x-axis at (4, 0). Try another example.

If you know that $x = -3$...

Then you know...

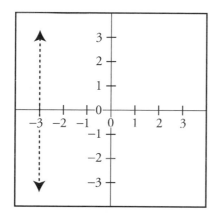

Every point on the dotted line has an x-coordinate of -3.

Points on the dotted line include $(-3, 1)$, $(-3, -7)$, $(-3, 100)$, and so on. In general, if you know the x-coordinate of a point and not the y-coordinate, then all you can say about the point is that it lies somewhere on a vertical line.

The x-coordinate still indicates left-right position. If you fix that position but not the up-down position, then the point can only move up and down—forming a vertical line.

Now imagine that all you know is the y-coordinate of a number. Say you know that $y = -2$. How could you represent this on the coordinate plane? In other words, what are all the points for which $y = -2$?

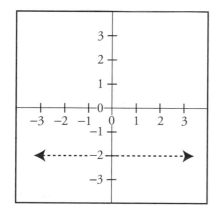

Every point 2 units below 0 fits this condition. These points form a horizontal line. You don't know anything about the x-coordinate, which could be any number. All the points along the horizontal dotted line have different x-coordinates but the same y-coordinate, which equals -2. For instance, $(-3, -2)$, $(-2, -2)$, and $(50, -2)$ are all on the line.

Try another example. If you know that $y = 1$…

Then you know…

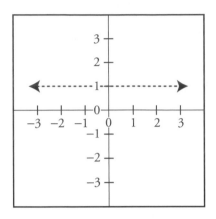

Every point on the dotted line has a y-coordinate of 1.

If you know the y-coordinate but not the x-coordinate, then you know the point lies somewhere on a horizontal line.

Check Your Skills

Draw a coordinate plane and plot the following lines.

3. $x = 6$
4. $y = -2$
5. $x = 0$

Answers can be found on pages 163–164.

Knowing Ranges

Now try having even less information. Instead of knowing the actual x-coordinate, see what happens if all you know is a range of possible values for x. What do you do if all you know is that $x > 0$? To answer that, return to the number line for a moment. As you saw earlier, if $x > 0$, then the target is anywhere to the right of 0:

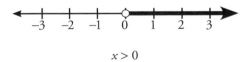

$x > 0$

Now look at the coordinate plane. All you know is that x is greater than 0. And you don't know *anything* about y, which could be any number.

How do you show all the possible points? You can shade in part of the coordinate plane: the part to the right of 0.

MANHATTAN
PREP

If you know that $x > 0$…

Then you know…

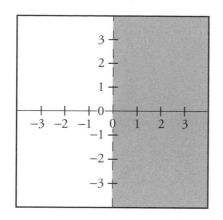

Every point in the shaded region has an x-coordinate greater than 0.

Now say that all you know is $y < 0$. Then you can shade in the bottom half of the coordinate plane (shown below)—where the y-coordinate is less than 0. The x-coordinate can be anything. Notice that the dashed line in the plane below indicates that y cannot be 0. It must be below the dashed line.

If you know that $y < 0$…

Then you know…

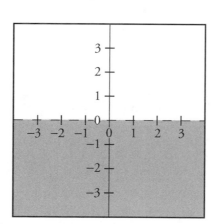

Every point in the shaded region has a y-coordinate less than 0.

Finally, if you know information about both x and y, then you can narrow down the shaded region.

7

If you know that $x > 0$ AND $y < 0$...

Then you know...

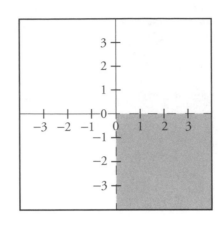

The only place where x is greater than 0 AND y is less than 0 is the bottom right quarter of the plane. So you know that the point lies somewhere in the bottom right quarter of the coordinate plane.

The four quarters of the coordinate plane are called **quadrants**. Each quadrant corresponds to a different combination of signs of x and y. The quadrants are always numbered as shown below, starting on the top right and going counter-clockwise:

Check Your Skills

6. In which quadrant do each of the following points lie?

    1. (1, −2)   2. (−4.6, 7)   3. (−1, −2.5)   4. (3, 3)

7. Which quadrant or quadrants are indicated by the following?

    1. $x < 0, y > 0$ 2. $x < 0, y < 0$ 3. $y > 0$ 4. $x < 0$

Answers can be found on page 164.

Reading a Graph

If you see a point on a coordinate plane, you can read off its coordinates as follows. To find an *x*-coordinate, drop an imaginary line down to the *x*-axis (if the point is above the *x*-axis) or draw a line up to the *x*-axis (if the point is below the *x*-axis) and read off the number. For example:

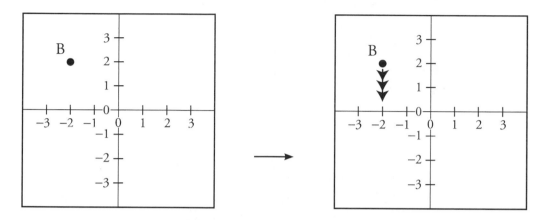

The line hits the *x*-axis at −2, which means the *x*-coordinate of your point is −2. Now, to find the *y*-coordinate, you employ a similar technique, only now you draw a horizontal line instead of a vertical line:

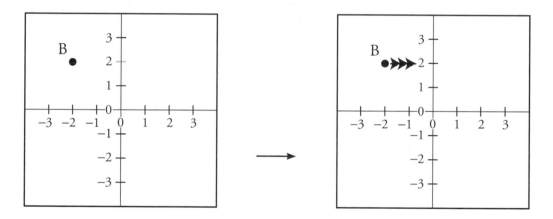

The line touched the *y*-axis at 2, which means the *y*-coordinate of the point is 2. Thus, the coordinates of point B are (−2, 2).

7

Now suppose that you know the target is on a slanted line in the plane. You can read coordinates off of this slanted line. Try this problem on your own first:

On the line shown, what is the *y*-coordinate of the point that has an *x*-coordinate of −4?

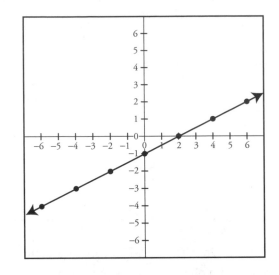

To answer this question, think about reading the coordinates of a point. You went from the point to the axes. Here, you will go from the axis that you know (here, the *x*-axis) to the line that contains the point, and then to the *y*-axis (the axis you don't know):

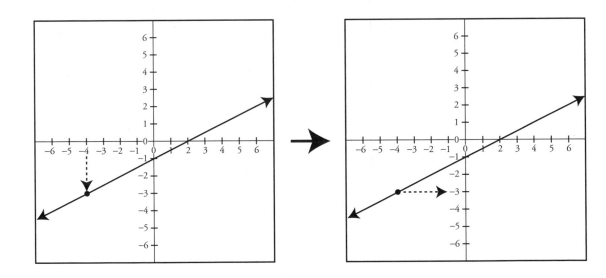

So the point on the line that has an *x*-coordinate of −4 has a *y*-coordinate of −3.

This method of locating points applies equally well to any shape or curve you may encounter on a coordinate plane. Try this next problem:

On the curve shown, what is the value of y when $x = 2$?

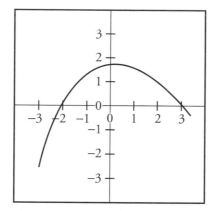

Once again, you know the x-coordinate, so draw a line from the x-axis (where you know the coordinate) to the curve, and then draw a line to the y-axis:

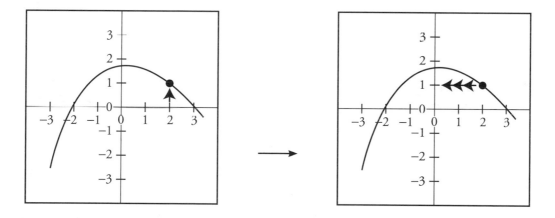

On the curve shown, the point that has an x-coordinate of 2 has a y-coordinate of 1.

Note that the GRE will mathematically define each line or curve, so you will never be forced to guess visually where a point falls. In fact, if more specific information is *not* given for a coordinate problem on the GRE, you *cannot* infer the location of a point based solely on visual cues. This discussion is *only* meant as an exercise to convey how to use any graphical representation.

7

Check Your Skills

8. On the following graph, what is the *y*-coordinate of the point on the line that has an *x*-coordinate of −3?

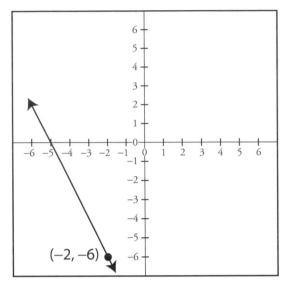

(−2, −6)

The answer can be found on page 164.

Plotting a Relationship

The most frequent use of the coordinate plane is to display a relationship between *x* and *y*. Often, this relationship is expressed this way: if you tell me *x*, I can tell you *y*.

As an equation, this sort of relationship looks like this:

y = some expression involving *x*   Another way of saying this is "We have *y* in terms of *x*."

Examples: $y = 2x + 1$ If you plug in a number for *x* in any of these
                 $y = x^2 - 3x + 2$ equations, you can calculate a value for *y*.
                 $y = \dfrac{x}{x + 2}$

For example, take $y = 2x + 1$. You can generate a set of *y*'s by plugging in various values of *x*. Start by making a table:

x	$y = 2x + 1$
−1	$y = 2(-1) + 1 = -1$
0	$y = 2(0) + 1 = 1$
1	$y = 2(1) + 1 = 3$
2	$y = 2(2) + 1 = 5$

Now that you have some values, see what you can do with them. You can say that when *x* equals 0, *y* equals 1. These two values form a pair. You express this connection by plotting the point (0, 1) on the coordinate plane. Similarly, you can plot all the other points that represent an *x-y* pair from your table:

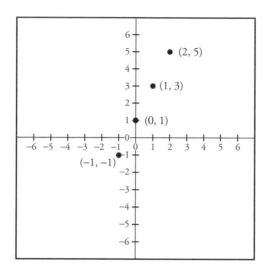

You might notice that these points seem to lie on a straight line. You're right—they do. In fact, any point that you can generate using the relationship $y = 2x + 1$ will also lie on the line:

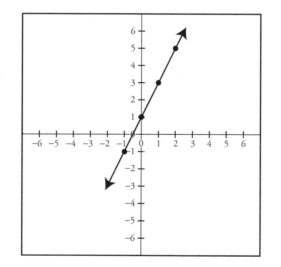

This line is the graphical representation of $y = 2x + 1$.

So now you can talk about equations in visual terms. In fact, that's what lines and curves on the coordinate plane are—they represent all the (*x*, *y*) pairs that make an equation true. Take a look at the following example:

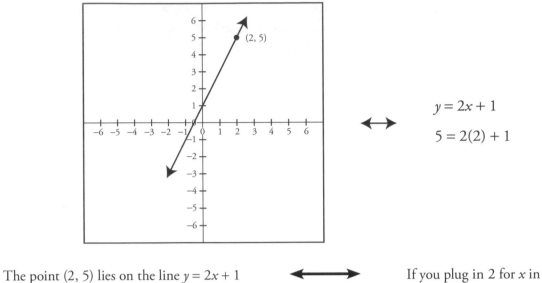

$$y = 2x + 1$$
$$5 = 2(2) + 1$$

The point (2, 5) lies on the line $y = 2x + 1$ ⟷ If you plug in 2 for x in $y = 2x + 1$, you get 5 for y.

You can even speak more generally, using variables:

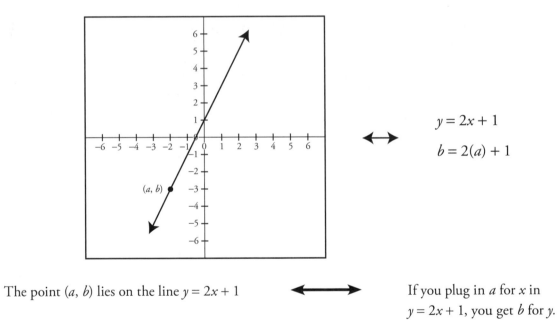

$$y = 2x + 1$$
$$b = 2(a) + 1$$

The point (a, b) lies on the line $y = 2x + 1$ ⟷ If you plug in a for x in $y = 2x + 1$, you get b for y.

Check Your Skills

9. True or False? The point (9, 21) is on the line $y = 2x + 1$.
10. True or False? The point (4, 14) is on the curve $y = x^2 - 2$.

Answers can be found on page 165.

Lines in the Plane

The relationship $y = 2x + 1$ formed a line in the coordinate plane, as you saw. You can actually generalize this relationship. *Any* relationship of the following form represents a line:

$y = mx + b$ *m* and *b* represent numbers (positive, negative, or 0)

For instance, in the equation $y = 2x + 1$, you can see that $m = 2$ and $b = 1$:

Lines		Not Lines
$y = 3x - 2$	$m = 3, b = -2$	$y = x^2$
$y = -x + 4$	$m = -1, b = 4$	$y = \dfrac{1}{x}$
These are called linear equations.		These equations are not linear.

The numbers *m* and *b* have special meanings when you are dealing with linear equations. First, *m* = **slope**. This tells you how steep the line is and whether the line is rising or falling:

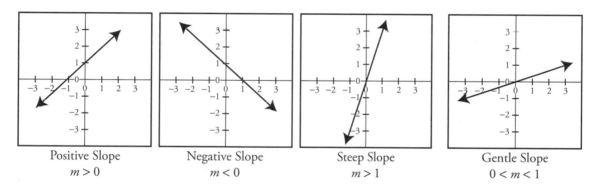

Positive Slope	Negative Slope	Steep Slope	Gentle Slope
$m > 0$	$m < 0$	$m > 1$	$0 < m < 1$

Next, *b* = **y-intercept**. This tells you where the line crosses the *y*-axis. Any line or curve crosses the *y*-axis when $x = 0$. To find the *y*-intercept, plug in 0 for *x* in the equation:

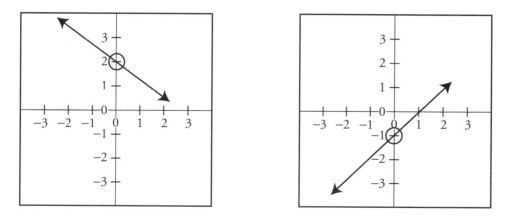

By recognizing linear equations and identifying *m* and *b*, you can plot a line more quickly than by plotting several points on the line.

<u>Check Your Skills</u>

Find the slope and y-intercept of the following lines.

11. $y = 3x + 4$
12. $2y = 5x - 12$

Answers can be found on page 165.

Now the question becomes, how do you use m and b to sketch a line? Plot the line $y = \frac{1}{2}x - 2$.

The easiest way to begin graphing a line is to begin with the y-intercept. You know that the line crosses the y-axis at $y = -2$, so begin by plotting that point on your coordinate plane:

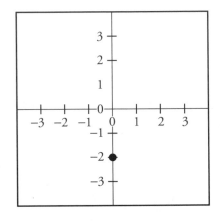

Now you need to figure out how to use slope in order to finish drawing your line. Every slope, whether an integer or a fraction, should be thought of as a fraction. In this equation, m is $\frac{1}{2}$. Look at the parts of the fraction and see what they can tell you about your slope:

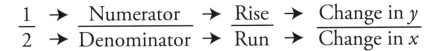

$$\frac{1}{2} \ \rightarrow \ \frac{\text{Numerator}}{\text{Denominator}} \ \rightarrow \ \frac{\text{Rise}}{\text{Run}} \ \rightarrow \ \frac{\text{Change in } y}{\text{Change in } x}$$

The numerator of your fraction tells you how many units you want to move in the y direction—in other words, how far up or down you want to move. The denominator tells you how many units you want to move in the x direction—in other words, how far left or right you want to move. For this particular equation, the slope is $\frac{1}{2}$, which means you want to move up 1 unit and right 2 units:

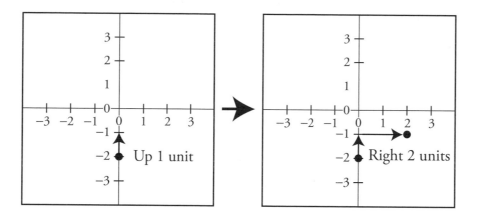

After you went up 1 unit and right 2 units, you ended up at the point $(2, -1)$. What that means is that the point $(2, -1)$ is also a solution to the equation $y = \frac{1}{2}x - 2$. In fact, you can plug in the x value and solve for y to check that you did this correctly:

$$y = \frac{1}{2}x - 2 \quad \rightarrow \quad y = \frac{1}{2}(2) - 2 \quad \rightarrow \quad y = 1 - 2 \quad \rightarrow \quad y = -1$$

What this means is that you can use the slope to generate points and draw your line. If you go up another 1 unit and right another 2 units, you will end up with another point that appears on the line. Although you could keep doing this indefinitely, in reality, with only 2 points you can figure out what your line looks like. Now all you need to do is draw the line that connects the 2 points you have, and you're done:

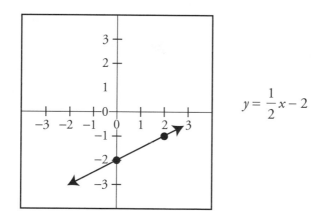

$$y = \frac{1}{2}x - 2$$

This line is the graphical representation of $y = \frac{1}{2}x - 2$.

Try another one. Graph the equation $y = \left(-\frac{3}{2}\right)x + 4$.

Once again, the best way to start is to plot the *y*-intercept. In this equation, $b = 4$, so you know the line crosses the *y*-axis at the point (0, 4):

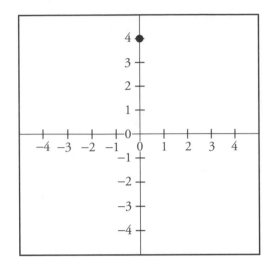

Now you can use the slope to find a second point. This time, the slope is $-\dfrac{3}{2}$, which is a negative slope. While positive slopes go up and to the right, negative slopes go down and to the right. You might think of it this way: if the "rise" is negative, that is like a "drop" or "fall." Now, to find the next point, you need to go *down* 3 units and right 2 units:

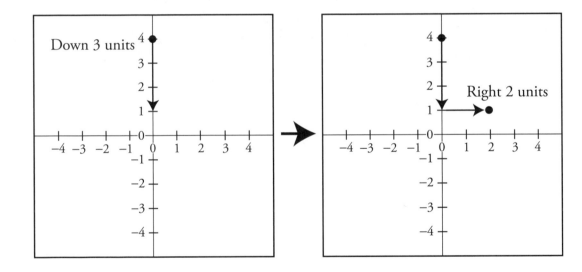

That means that (2, 1) is another point on the line. Now that you have two points, you can draw your line:

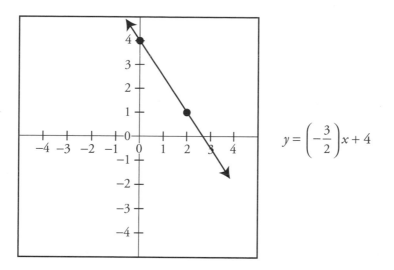

$$y = \left(-\frac{3}{2}\right)x + 4$$

Check Your Skills

13. Draw a coordinate plane and graph the line $y = 2x - 4$. Identify the slope and the y-intercept.

The answer can be found on page 165.

The Intercepts of a Line

A point where a line intersects a coordinate axis is called an **intercept**. There are two types of intercepts: the x-intercept, where the line intersects the x-axis, and the y-intercept, where the line intersects the y-axis.

The x-intercept is expressed using the ordered pair $(x, 0)$, where x is the point where the line intersects the x-axis. **The x-intercept is the point on the line at which $y = 0$.** In this diagram, the x-intercept is −4, as expressed by the ordered pair (−4, 0).

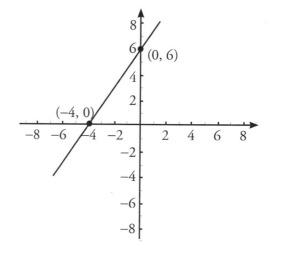

The y-intercept is expressed using the ordered pair $(0, y)$, where y is the point where the line intersects the y-axis. **The y-intercept is the point on the line at which $x = 0$.** In this diagram, the y-intercept is 6, as expressed by the ordered pair (0, 6).

To find x-intercepts, plug in 0 for y. To find y-intercepts, plug in 0 for x.

7

<u>Check Your Skills</u>

14. What are the x- and y-intercepts of the equation $x - 2y = 8$?

The answer can be found on pages 165–166.

The Intersection of Two Lines

Recall that a line in the coordinate plane is defined by a linear equation relating x and y. That is, if a point (x, y) lies on the line, then those values of x and y satisfy the equation. For instance, the point $(3, 2)$ lies on the line defined by the equation $y = 4x - 10$, since the equation is true when you plug in $x = 3$ and $y = 2$:

$$y = 4x - 10$$
$$2 = 4(3) - 10 = 12 - 10$$
$$2 = 2 \quad \text{True}$$

On the other hand, the point $(7, 5)$ does not lie on that line, because the equation is false when you plug in $x = 7$ and $y = 5$:

$$y = 4x - 10$$
$$5 = 4(7) - 10 = 28 - 10 = 18? \quad \text{False}$$

So, what does it mean when two lines intersect in the coordinate plane? It means that at the point of intersection, BOTH equations representing the lines are true. That is, the pair of numbers (x, y) that represents the point of intersection solves BOTH equations. Finding this point of intersection is equivalent to solving a system of two linear equations. You can find the intersection by using algebra more easily than by graphing the two lines. Try this example:

At what point does the line represented by $y = 4x - 10$ intersect the line represented by $2x + 3y = 26$?

Since $y = 4x - 10$, replace y in the second equation with $4x - 10$ and solve for x:

$$2x + 3(4x - 10) = 26$$
$$2x + 12x - 30 = 26$$
$$14x = 56$$
$$x = 4$$

Now solve for y. You can use either equation, but the first one is more convenient:

$$y = 4x - 10$$
$$y = 4(4) - 10$$
$$y = 16 - 10 = 6$$

Thus, the point of intersection of the two lines is $(4, 6)$.

If two lines in a plane do not intersect, then the lines are parallel. If this is the case, there is *no* pair of numbers (*x*, *y*) that satisfies both equations at the same time.

Two linear equations can represent two lines that intersect at a single point, or they can represent parallel lines that never intersect. There is one other possibility: the two equations might represent the same line. In this case, infinitely many points (*x*, *y*) along the line satisfy the two equations (one of which must actually be the other equation in disguise).

The Distance Between Two Points

The distance between any two points in the coordinate plane can be calculated by using the Pythagorean theorem. For example:

What is the distance between the points (1, 3) and (7, −5)?

First, draw a right triangle connecting the points.

Second, find the lengths of the two legs of the triangle by calculating the rise and the run:

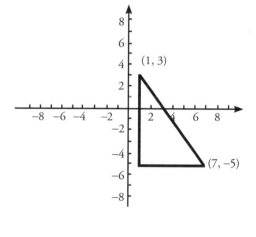

The *y*-coordinate changes from 3 to −5,
a difference of 8 (the vertical leg).

The *x*-coordinate changes from 1 to 7,
a difference of 6 (the horizontal leg).

Third, use the Pythagorean theorem to calculate the length of the diagonal, which is the distance between the points:

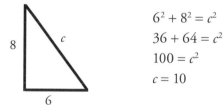

$$6^2 + 8^2 = c^2$$
$$36 + 64 = c^2$$
$$100 = c^2$$
$$c = 10$$

The distance between the two points is 10 units.

Alternatively, to find the hypotenuse, you may have recognized this triangle as a variation of a 3–4–5 triangle (specifically, a 6–8–10 triangle).

Check Your Skills

15. What is the distance between (−2, −4) and (3, 8)?

The answer can be found on page 166.

MANHATTAN
PREP

Check Your Skills Answer Key

1.

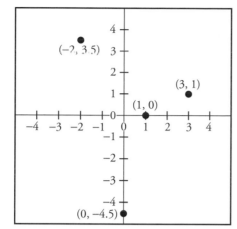

2.   1. (2, −1): **E**

      2. (−1.5, −3): **C**

      3. (−1, 2): **B**

      4. (3, 2): **D**

      5. (2, 3): **A**

3.

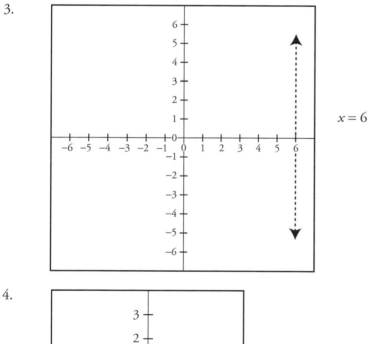

$x = 6$

4.

$y = −2$

5.

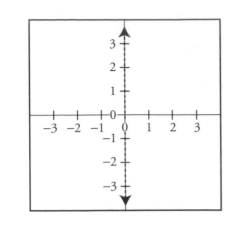

$x = 0$ is the y-axis.

6.   1. $(1, -2)$ is in **Quadrant IV**
      2. $(-4.6, 7)$ is in **Quadrant II**
      3. $(-1, -2.5)$ is in **Quadrant III**
      4. $(3, 3)$ is in **Quadrant I**

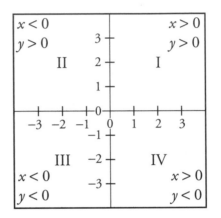

7.   1. $x < 0$, $y > 0$ indicates **Quadrant II**
      2. $x < 0$, $y < 0$ indicates **Quadrant III**
      3. $y > 0$ indicates **Quadrants I and II**
      4. $x < 0$ indicates **Quadrants II and III**

8. The point on the line with $x = -3$
has a y-coordinate of -4.

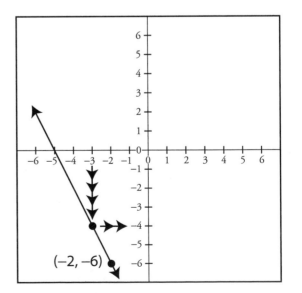

(−2, −6)

MANHATTAN
PREP

9. **False:** The relationship is $y = 2x + 1$, and the point you are testing is (9, 21). So plug in 9 for x and see what you get: $y = 2(9) + 1 = 19$. The point (9, 21) does not lie on the line.

10. **True:** The relationship is $y = x^2 - 2$, and the point you are testing is (4, 14). So plug in 4 for x and see what you get: $y = (4)^2 - 2 = 14$. The point (4, 14) lies on the curve.

11. **Slope is 3, y-intercept is 4:** The equation $y = 3x + 4$ is already in $y = mx + b$ form, so you can directly find the slope and y-intercept. The slope is 3, and the y-intercept is 4.

12. **Slope is 2.5, y-intercept is −6:** To find the slope and y-intercept of a line, you need the equation to be in $y = mx + b$ form. You need to divide the original equation by 2 to make that happen. So $2y = 5x - 12$ becomes $y = 2.5x - 6$. So the slope is 2.5 (or 5/2) and the y-intercept is −6.

13. **Slope is 2, y-intercept is −4:**

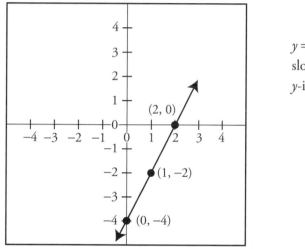

$y = 2x - 4$
slope = 2
y-intercept = −4

14. **x-intercept is 8, y-intercept is −4:**

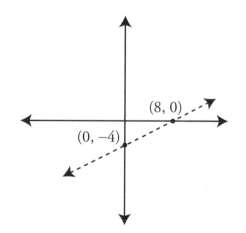

The line is drawn on the coordinate plane above, but you can also answer this question using algebra.

To determine the *x*-intercept, set *y* equal to 0, then solve for *x*:

$x - 2y = 8$
$y = 0$
$x - 0 = 8$
$x = 8$

To determine the *y*-intercept, set *x* equal to 0, then solve for *y*:

$x - 2y = 8$
$x = 0$
$0 - 2y = 8$
$-2y = 8$
$y = -4$

15. **13:**

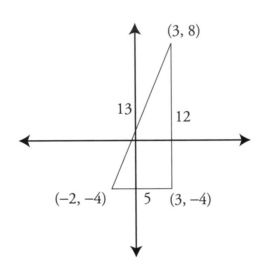

The illustration above shows the two points. A right triangle has been constructed by finding a point directly below (3, 8) and directly to the right of (−2, −4). This right triangle has legs of 5 (the change from −2 to 3) and 12 (the change from −4 to 8). You can plug those values into the Pythagorean theorem and solve for the hypotenuse:

$A^2 + B^2 = C^2$
$5^2 + 12^2 = C^2$
$25 + 144 = C^2$
$C^2 = 169$
$C = \sqrt{169} = 13$

Alternatively, you could recognize the common Pythagorean triple 5–12–13.

Problem Set

1. A line has the equation $y = 3x + 7$. At which point will this line intersect the y-axis?

2. A line has the equation $x = \dfrac{y}{80} - 20$. At which point will this line intersect the x-axis?

3   A line has the equation $x = -2y + z$. If $(3, 2)$ is a point on the line, what is z?

4. A line is represented by the equation $y = zx + 18$. If this line intersects the x-axis at $(-3, 0)$, what is z?

5. A line has a slope of 1/6 and intersects the x-axis at $(-24, 0)$. Where does this line intersect the y-axis?

6. Which quadrants, if any, do not contain any points on the line represented by $x - y = 18$?

7. Which quadrants, if any, do not contain any points on the line represented by $x = 10y$?

8. Which quadrants contain points on the line $y = \dfrac{x}{1,000} + 1,000,000$?

9. Which quadrants contain points on the line represented by $x + 18 = 2y$?

10. What is the equation of the line shown to the right?

11. What is the intersection point of the lines defined by the equations $2x + y = 7$ and $3x - 2y = 21$?

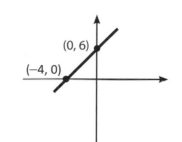

(0, 6)

(−4, 0)

12.

Quantity A	**Quantity B**
The y-intercept of the line	The x-intercept of the line
$y = \dfrac{3}{2}x - 2$	$y = \dfrac{3}{2}x - 2$

7

13.

Quantity A	**Quantity B**
The slope of the line	The slope of the line
$2x + 5y = 10$	$5x + 2y = 10$

14.

Quantity A	**Quantity B**
The distance between points	The distance between points
$(0, 9)$ and $(-2, 0)$	$(3, 9)$ and $(10, 3)$

Solutions

1. **(0, 7):** A line intersects the y-axis at the y-intercept. Since this equation is written in slope-intercept form, the y-intercept is easy to identify: 7. Thus, the line intersects the y-axis at the point (0, 7).

2. **(−20, 0):** A line intersects the x-axis at the x-intercept, or when the y-coordinate is equal to 0. Substitute 0 for y and solve for x:

$$x = 0 - 20$$
$$x = -20$$

3. **7:** Substitute the coordinates (3, 2) for x and y and solve for z:

$$3 = -2(2) + z$$
$$3 = -4 + z$$
$$z = 7$$

4. **6:** Substitute the coordinates (−3, 0) for x and y and solve for z:

$$0 = z(-3) + 18$$
$$3z = 18$$
$$z = 6$$

5. **(0, 4):** Use the information given to find the equation of the line:

$$y = \frac{1}{6}x + b$$
$$0 = \frac{1}{6}(-24) + b$$
$$0 = -4 + b$$
$$b = 4$$

The variable b represents the y-intercept. Therefore, the line intersects the y-axis at (0, 4).

6. **II:** First, rewrite the line in slope-intercept form:

$$y = x - 18$$

Find the intercepts by setting x to 0 and y to 0:

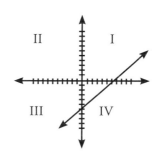

$$y = 0 - 18 \qquad\qquad 0 = x - 18$$
$$y = -18 \qquad\qquad x = 18$$

Plot the points: (0, −18), and (18, 0). From the sketch, you can see that the line does not pass through quadrant II.

7. **II and IV:** First, rewrite the line in slope-intercept form:

$$y = \frac{x}{10}$$

Notice from the equation that the *y*-intercept of the line is (0,0). This means that the line crosses the *y*-intercept at the origin, so the *x*- and *y*-intercepts are the same. To find another point on the line, substitute any convenient number for *x*; in this case, 10 would be a convenient, or "smart," number:

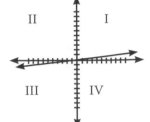

$$y = \frac{10}{10} = 1 \qquad \text{The point (10, 1) is on the line.}$$

Plot the points: (0, 0) and (10, 1). From the sketch, you can see that the line does not pass through quadrants II and IV.

8. **I, II, and III:** The line is already written in slope-intercept form:

$$y = \frac{x}{1,000} + 1,000,000$$

Find the intercepts by setting *x* to 0 and *y* to 0:

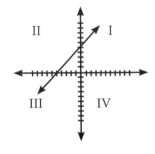

$$0 = \frac{x}{1,000} + 1,000,000 \qquad y = \frac{0}{1,000} + 1,000,000$$

$$x = -1,000,000,000 \qquad y = 1,000,000$$

Plot the points: (−1,000,000,000, 0) and (0, 1,000,000). From the sketch, which is obviously not to scale, you can see that the line passes through quadrants I, II, and III.

9. **I, II, and III:** First, rewrite the line in slope-intercept form:

$$y = \frac{x}{2} + 9$$

Find the intercepts by setting *x* to 0 and *y* to 0:

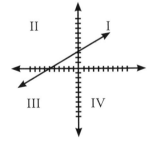

$$0 = \frac{x}{2} + 9 \qquad y = \frac{0}{2} + 9$$

$$x = -18 \qquad y = 9$$

Plot the points: (−18, 0) and (0, 9). From the sketch, you can see that the line passes through quadrants I, II, and III.

10. $y = \dfrac{3}{2}x + 6$: First, calculate the slope of the line:

$$\text{slope} = \frac{\text{rise}}{\text{run}} = \frac{6-0}{0-(-4)} = \frac{6}{4} = \frac{3}{2}$$

You can see from the graph that the line crosses the y-axis at $(0, 6)$. The equation of the line is:

$$y = \frac{3}{2}x + 6$$

11. **(5, −3):** To find the coordinates of the point of intersection, solve the system of two linear equations. You could turn both equations into slope-intercept form and set them equal to each other, but it is easier to multiply the first equation by 2 and then add the second equation:

$2x + y = 7$	(first equation)		$7x = 35$	(sum of previous two eqations)
$4x + 2y = 14$	(first equation multipied by 2)		$x = 5$	
$3x - 2y = 21$	(second equation)			

Now plug $x = 5$ into either equation:

$2x + y = 7$	(first equation)		$10 + y = 7$
$2(5) + y = 7$			$y = -3$

Thus, the point $(5, -3)$ is the point of intersection. There is no need to graph the two lines to find the point of intersection.

12. **(B):**

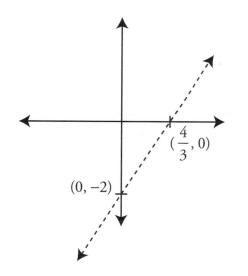

The line is illustrated on the coordinate plane above. Because the equation is already in slope intercept form ($y = mx + b$), you can read the y-intercept directly from the b position, and use the slope to determine the x-intercept. A slope of 3/2 means that the line corresponding to this equation will rise 3 for every 2 that it runs. You don't need to determine the exact x-intercept to see that it is positive, and so greater than −2.

Alternatively, you could set each variable equal to 0 and determine the intercepts.

To determine the y-intercept, set x equal to 0, then solve for y:

$$y = \frac{3}{2}x - 2$$

$$y = \frac{3}{2}(0) - 2$$

$$y = 0 - 2 = -2$$

To determine the x-intercept, set y equal to 0, then solve for x:

$$y = \frac{3}{2}x - 2$$

$$(0) = \frac{3}{2}x - 2$$

$$2 = \frac{3}{2}x$$

$$\frac{4}{3} = x$$

Quantity A	**Quantity B**
The y-intercept of the line	The x-intercept of the line
-2	$\dfrac{4}{3}$

Therefore, **Quantity B is greater**.

13. **(A):** The best method would be to put each equation into slope-intercept form ($y = mx + b$) and see which has the greater value for m, which represents the slope. Start with the equation in Quantity A:

$$2x + 5y = 10$$

$$5y = -2x + 10$$

$$y = -\frac{2}{5}x + 2$$

Quantity A	**Quantity B**
The slope of the line $2x + 5y = 10$ is $-\dfrac{2}{5}$	The slope of the line $5x + 2y = 10$

Now find the slope of the equation in Quantity B:

MANHATTAN
PREP

$$5x + 2y = 10$$
$$2y = -5x + 10$$
$$y = -\frac{5}{2}x + 5$$

Quantity A	**Quantity B**
$-\dfrac{2}{5}$	The slope of the line $5x + 2y = 10$ is $-\dfrac{5}{2}$

Be careful. Remember that $-\dfrac{2}{5} > -\dfrac{5}{2}$. Therefore, **Quantity A is greater**.

14. **C:**

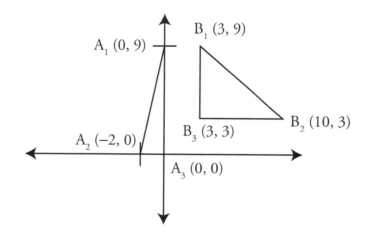

The illustration above shows the two points from Quantity A, here labeled A_1 and A_2, and the two points from Quantity B, here labeled B_1 and B_2. You can construct a right triangle from the A values by finding a point $(0, 0)$ directly below A_1 and directly to the right of A_2. This right triangle has legs of 2 (the change from -2 to 0) and 9 (the change from 0 to 9). You can plug those values into the Pythagorean theorem and solve for the hypotenuse:

$$a^2 + b^2 = c^2$$
$$(2)^2 + (9)^2 = c^2$$
$$4 + 81 = c^2$$
$$c^2 = 85$$
$$c = \sqrt{85}$$

Quantity A	**Quantity B**
The distance between points $(0, 9)$ and $(-2, 0) = \sqrt{85}$	The distance between points $(3, 9)$ and $(10, 3)$

You can construct a right triangle from the B values by finding a point (3, 3) directly below B_1 and directly to the left of B_2. This right triangle has legs of 7 (the change from 3 to 10) and 6 (the change from 3 to 9). You can plug those values into the Pythagorean theorem and solve for the hypotenuse:

$a^2 + b^2 = c^2$

$(7)^2 + (6)^2 = c^2$

$49 + 36 = c^2$

$c^2 = 85$

$c = \sqrt{85}$

Quantity A	**Quantity B**
The distance between points	The distance between points (3, 9)
$(0, 9)$ and $(-2, 0) = \sqrt{85}$	and $(10, 3) = \sqrt{85}$

Therefore, **the two quantities are equal**.

7

Chapter 8
of Geometry

Drill Sets

In This Chapter...

Chapter Review: Drill Sets

Chapter Review: Drill Sets

Drill Set 1

1.   The radius of a circle is 4. What is its area?
2.   The diameter of a circle is 7. What is its circumference?
3.   The radius of a circle is 3. What is its circumference?
4.   The area of a circle is 36π. What is its radius?
5.   The circumference of a circle is 18π. What is its area?

6.   The area of a circle is 100π. What is its circumference?
7.   The diameter of a circle is 16. Calculate its radius, circumference, and area.
8.   Which circle has a larger area? Circle A has a circumference of 6π and circle B has an area of 8π.
9.   Which has a larger area? Circle C has a diameter of 10 and circle D has a circumference of 12π.
10. A circle initially has an area of 4π. If the radius is doubled, the new area is how many times as large as the original area?

11. A sector has a central angle of $90°$. If the sector has a radius of 8, what is the area of the sector?
12. A sector has a central angle of $30°$. If the sector has a radius of 6, what is the arc length of the sector?
13. A sector has an arc length of 7π and a radius of 7. What is the central angle of the sector?
14. A sector has a central angle of $270°$. If the sector has a radius of 4, what is the area of the sector?
15. A sector has an area of 24π and a radius of 12. What is the central angle of the sector?

16. The area of a sector is $\dfrac{1}{10}$ the area of the full circle. What is the central angle of the sector?

17. What is the perimeter of a sector with a radius of 5 and a central angle of $72°$?
18. A sector has a radius of 8 and an area of 8π. What is the arc length of the sector?
19. A sector has an arc length of $\dfrac{\pi}{2}$ and a central angle of $45°$. What is the radius of the sector?

20. Which of the following two sectors has a larger area? Sector A has a radius of 4 and a central angle of $90°$. Sector B has a radius of 6 and a central angle of $45°$.

Drill Set 2

1.   A triangle has two sides with lengths of 5 and 11, respectively. What is the range of values for the length of the third side?
2.   In a right triangle, the length of one of the legs is 3 and the length of the hypotenuse is 5. What is the length of the other leg?

3. What is the area of triangle *DEF*?

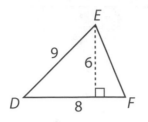

4. Which side of Triangle *GHI* has the longest length?

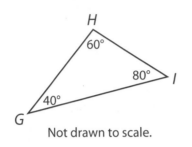

Not drawn to scale.

5. What is the value of *x*?

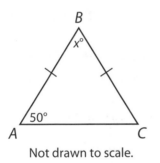

Not drawn to scale.

6. Two sides of a triangle have lengths 4 and 8. Which of the following are possible side lengths of the third side? (More than one may apply.)

    a. 2   b. 4   c. 6   d. 8

7. *DFG* is a straight line. What is the value of *x*?

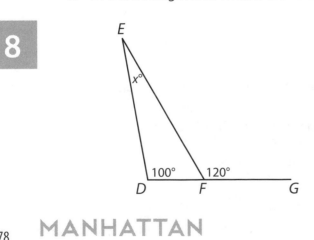

8. Isosceles triangle *ABC* has a side with a length of 3 and a side with a length of 9. What is the length of the third side?

9. Which of the following could be the length of side *AB*, if $x < y < z$? (Refer to the figure below.)

   a. 6   b. 10   c. 14

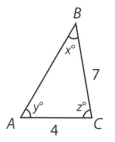

10. What is the area of right triangle *ABC*?

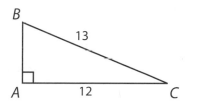

11. What is the perimeter of triangle *ABC*?

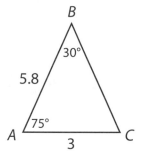

12. The area of right triangle *ABC* is 15. What is the length of hypotenuse *BC*?

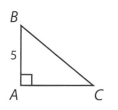

8

13. What is the length of side *HI*?

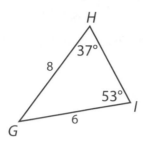

14. Which triangle has the greatest perimeter?

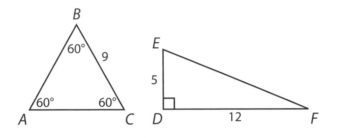

15. If *ZW* has a length of 3 and *XZ* has a length of 6, what is the area of triangle *XYZ*?

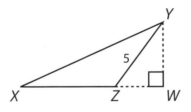

Drill Set 3

1. What is the perimeter of parallelogram *ABCD*?

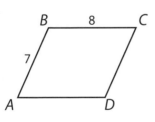

2. What is the area of parallelogram *EFGH*?

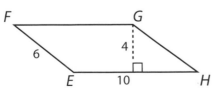

3. The two parallelograms pictured below have the same perimeter. What is the length of side *EH*?

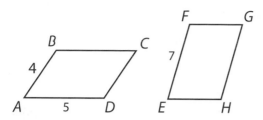

4. In parallelogram *ABCD*, Triangle *ABC* has an area of 12. What is the area of triangle *ACD*?

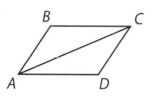

5. Rectangle *WXYZ* and rectangle *OPQR* have equal areas. What is the length of side *PQ*?

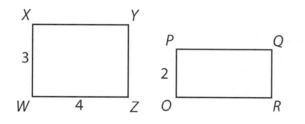

6. What is the area of rectangle *ABCD*?

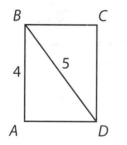

7. In rectangle *ABCD*, the area of triangle *ABC* is 30. What is the length of diagonal *AC*?

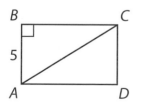

8

8. Rectangles *ABCD* and *EFGH* have equal areas. What is the length of side *FG*?

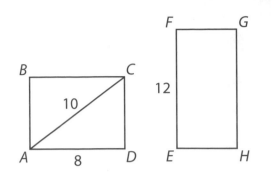

9. A rectangle has a perimeter of 10 and an area of 6. What are the length and width of the rectangle?

10. Triangle *ABC* and rectangle *JKLM* have equal areas. What is the perimeter of rectangle *JKLM*?

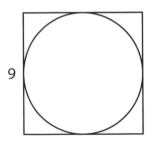

11. What is the perimeter of a square with an area of 25?

12. A rectangle and a square have the same area. The square has a perimeter of 32 and the rectangle has a length of 4. What is the width of the rectangle?

13. A circle is inscribed inside a square, so that the circle is tangent to all four sides of the square. The length of one of the sides of the square is 9. What is the area of the circle?

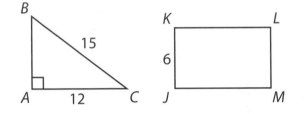

14. Square *ABCD* has an area of 49. What is the length of diagonal *AC*?

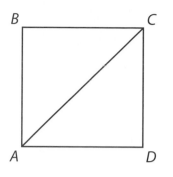

15. Right triangle *ABC* and rectangle *EFGH* have the same perimeter. What is the value of *x*?

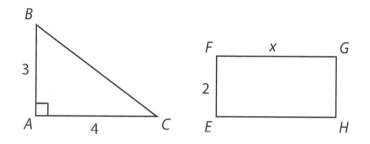

Drill Set 4

1. Draw a coordinate plane and plot the following points:

   1. (2, 3)   2. (−2, −1)   3. (−5, −6)   4. (4, −2.5)

2. What are the *x*- and *y*-coordinates of the following points?

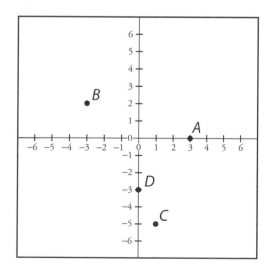

3. On the line pictured below, what is the *y*-coordinate of the point that has an
    x-coordinate of 3?

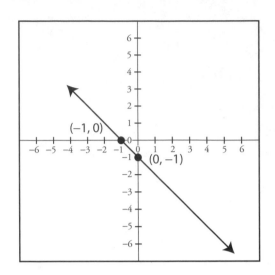

4. On the line pictured below, what is the *x*-coordinate of the point that has a *y*-coordinate
    of −4?

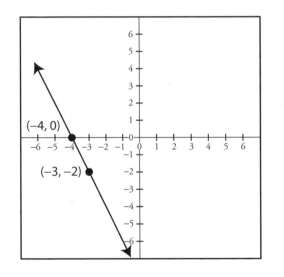

5. Does the point (3, −2) lie on the line $y = 2x - 8$?

6. Does the point (−3, 0) lie on the curve $y = x^2 - 3$?

7. For the line $y = 4x + 2$, what is the *y*-coordinate when $x = 3$?

8. What is the *y*-intercept of the line $y = -2x - 7$?

9. Graph the line $y = \dfrac{1}{3}x - 4$.

10. Graph the line $\dfrac{1}{2}y = -\dfrac{1}{2}x + 1$.

8

Drill Set Answers

Drill Set 1

1. **16π:** The area of a circle is πr^2, so the area of the circle is $\pi(4)^2$, which equals 16π.

2. **7π:** The circumference of a circle is $2\pi r$, or πd. You have the diameter, so the circumference equals $\pi(7)$, which equals 7π.

3. **6π:** The circumference of a circle is $2\pi r$, or πd. You have the radius, so circumference equals $2\pi(3)$, which equals 6π.

4. **6:** The area of a circle is πr^2, so $36\pi = \pi r^2$. You need to solve for r. Divide both sides by π, so $36 = r^2$. Take the square root of both sides, and $6 = r$. You can ignore the negative solution because distances cannot be negative.

5. **81π:** The connection between circumference and area is radius. You can use the circumference to solve for the radius: $18\pi = 2\pi r$, which means that $9 = r$. That means that area $= \pi(9)^2$, which equals 81π.

6. **20π:** The connection between circumference and area is radius. Using the area formula to solve for r, $100\pi = \pi r^2$, you get $r = 10$. That means that circumference $= 2\pi(10)$, which equals 20π.

7. **8, 16π, 64π:** $d = 2r$, so $16 = 2r$. The radius is 8, and the circumference is $2\pi r$, so circumference $= 2\pi(8) = 16\pi$. Area $= \pi r^2$, so area $= \pi(8)^2 = 64\pi$.

8. **Circle A:** To figure out which circle has a larger area, you need to find the area of circle A. If you know the circumference, then $6\pi = 2\pi r$, which means $r = 3$. If $r = 3$, then area $= \pi(3)^2 = 9\pi$. $9\pi > 8\pi$, so circle A has a larger area.

9. **Circle D:** You need to find the area of both circles. Start with circle C. If the diameter of circle C is 10, then the radius is 5. That means that area $= \pi(5)^2 = 25\pi$.

If the circumference of circle D is 12π, then $12\pi = 2\pi r$. $r = 6$. If $r = 6$, then area $= \pi(6)^2 = 36\pi$. $36\pi > 25\pi$, so circle D has the larger area.

10. **4 times:** To begin, you need to find the original radius of the circle. $4\pi = \pi r^2$, so $r = 2$. If you double the radius, the new radius is 4. A circle with a radius of 4 has an area of 16π. Since 16π is 4 times 4π, the new area is 4 times the original area.

11. **16π:** If the sector has a central angle of $90°$, then the sector is 1/4 of the circle, because $\dfrac{90}{360} = \dfrac{1}{4}$.

To find the area of the sector, you need to find the area of the whole circle first. The radius is 8, which means the area is $\pi(8)^2 = 64\pi$. Thus: $\dfrac{1}{4} \times 64\pi = 16\pi$. The area of the sector is 16π.

12. **π:** If the sector has a central angle of 30°, then it is 1/12 of the circle, because $\dfrac{30}{360} = \dfrac{1}{12}$. To find the arc length of the sector, you need to know the circumference of the entire circle. The radius of the circle is 6, so the circumference is $2\pi(6) = 12\pi$. That means that the arc length of the sector is $\dfrac{1}{12} \times 12\pi = \pi$.

13. **180°:** To find the central angle of the sector, you first need to find what fraction of the full circle the sector is. You have the arc length, so if you can find the circumference of the circle, you can figure out what fraction of the circle the sector is. The radius is 7, so the circumference is $2\pi(7) = 14\pi$. Then compare the arc length to the circumference: $\dfrac{7\pi}{14\pi} = \dfrac{1}{2}$. So the sector is 1/2 the full circle. That means that the central angle of the sector is $\dfrac{1}{2} \times 360° = 180°$. So the central angle is 180°.

14. **12π:** The sector is 3/4 of the circle, because $\dfrac{270°}{360°} = \dfrac{3}{4}$. To find the area of the sector, you need the area of the whole circle. The radius of the circle is 4, so the area is $\pi(4)^2 = 16\pi$. That means the area of the circle is $\dfrac{3}{4} \times 16\pi = 12\pi$.

15. **60°:** You first need to find the area of the whole circle. The radius is 12, which means the area is $\pi(12)^2 = 144\pi$. Then compare the sector area to the circle area: $\dfrac{24\pi}{144\pi} = \dfrac{1}{6}$, so the sector is 1/6th of the entire circle. That means that the central angle is 1/6th of 360. $\dfrac{1}{6} \times 360 = 60$, so the central angle is 60°.

16. **36°:** If the area of the sector is 1/10th of the area of the full circle, then the central angle will be 1/10th of the degree measure of the full circle. Because $\dfrac{1}{10} \times 360 = 36$, the central angle of the sector is 36°.

17. **$10 + 2\pi$:** To find the perimeter of a sector, you need to know the radius of the circle and the arc length of the sector:

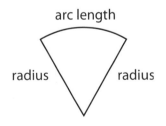

arc length

radius   radius

MANHATTAN
PREP

You know the radius is 5, so now you need to find the arc length. Begin by determining what fraction of the circle the sector is. The central angle of the sector is 72°, so the sector is 1/5th of the circle, because $\dfrac{72}{360} = \dfrac{1}{5}$. Now you need to find the circumference. The radius is 5, so the circumference of the circle is $2\pi(5) = 10\pi$. The arc length of the sector is 1/5th the circumference, or $\dfrac{1}{5} \times 10\pi = 2\pi$. So now your sector looks like this:

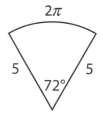

The perimeter of the sector is $10 + 2\pi$.

18. **2π**: You first need to find what fraction of the circle the sector is. You can do this by comparing areas. The radius of the circle is 8, so the area of the circle is $\pi(8)^2 = 64\pi$. That means the sector is 1/8th of the circle, because $\dfrac{8\pi}{64\pi} = \dfrac{1}{8}$. If you want to find the arc length of the sector, you need to know the circumference. The radius is 8, so the circumference is $2\pi(8) = 16\pi$. The sector is 1/8th of the circle, so the arc length will be 1/8th of the circumference, or $1/8 \times 16\pi = 2\pi$. The arc length of the sector is 2π.

19. **2**: If the sector has a central angle of 45°, then the sector is 1/8th of the circle, because $\dfrac{45}{360} = \dfrac{1}{8}$. If the sector is 1/8th of the circle, then that means the arc length of the sector is 1/8th of the circumference of the circle. That means that $\pi/2$ is 1/8th of the circumference. So the circumference is $\pi/2 \times 8 = 4\pi$. You know the formula for circumference, so you know that $4\pi = 2\pi r$. Divide both sides by 2π and you get $r = 2$. The radius of the sector is 2.

20. **Sector B**: You need to find the area of each circle. Sector A is 1/4th of its circle, because $\dfrac{90}{360} = \dfrac{1}{4}$. The radius is 4, so the area of the circle is $\pi(4)^2 = 16\pi$. That means the area of Sector A is 1/4th of 16π, or 4π.

Sector B is 1/8th of its circle, because $\dfrac{45}{360} = \dfrac{1}{8}$. The radius of Sector B is 6, so the area of the full circle is $\pi(6)^2 = 36\pi$. Sector B is 1/8th of the circle, so the area of Sector B is $\dfrac{1}{8} \times 36\pi = 4.5\pi$. The area of Sector B is 4.5π.

$4.5\pi > 4\pi$, so the area of Sector B is greater than the area of Sector A.

8

Drill Set 2

1. **6 < third side < 16:** The lengths of any two sides of a triangle must add up to more than the length of the third side. The third side must be less than 5 + 11 = 16. It must also be greater than 11 − 5 = 6. Therefore, 6 < third side < 16.

2. **4:** If you know the lengths of two sides of a right triangle, you can use the Pythagorean theorem to solve for the length of the third side. Remember that the hypotenuse must be the side labeled c in the equation $a^2 + b^2 = c^2$. That means that $(3)^2 + (b)^2 = (5)^2$. Thus: $9 + b^2 = 25$. Subtract 9 from each side to get $b^2 = 16$, so $b = 4$.

Alternatively, you can recognize the Pythagorean triple. This is a 3–4–5 triangle.

3. **24:** The area of a triangle is $\frac{1}{2}$(base) × (height). Remember that the base and the height must be perpendicular to each other. That means that in triangle *DEF*, side *DF* can act as the base, and the line dropping straight down from point *E* to touch side *DF* at a right angle can act as the height. Therefore, area = $\frac{1}{2}$(8) × (6) = 24.

4. **Side *GH*:** Remember that you shouldn't trust the picture scale, and should even expect distortion when a figure is explicitly labeled "Not drawn to scale." So although *GI* looks like the longest side, verify using the rules. In any triangle, the longest side will be opposite the largest angle. Angle *GIH* is the largest angle in the triangle, thus side *GH* is actually the longest side.

5. **80:** If you know the other two angles in a triangle, then you can find the third, because all three angles must add up to 180°. In triangle *ABC*, sides *AB* and *BC* are equal. That means their opposite angles are also equal. That means that angle *ACB* is also 50°.

Now that you know the other two angles, you can find angle *x*. You know that 50 + 50 + x = 180, so x = 80.

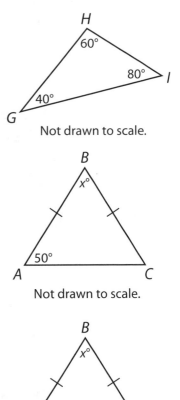

MANHATTAN
PREP

6. **(C)** and **(D):** The lengths of any two sides of a triangle must add up to more than the length of the third side. The third side must be less than $4 + 8 = 12$ and greater than $8 - 4 = 4$. So $4 <$ third side < 12. Only choices (C) and (D) are in that range.

7. **20°:** To find the value of x, you need to find the degree measures of the other two angles in Triangle *DEF*. You can make use of the fact that *DFG* is a straight line. Straight lines have a degree measure of 180, so angle $DFE + 120 = 180$, which means angle $DFE = 60°$.

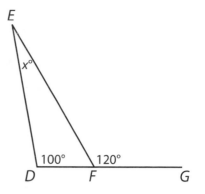

Now you can solve for x, because $100 + 60 + x = 180$. Solving for x, you get $x = 20$.

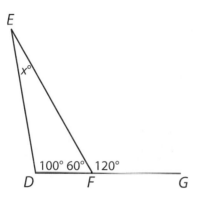

Alternatively, angle *EFG* is an exterior angle, equal to the sum of the two non-adjacent internal angles. $120 = x + 100$, so $x = 20$.

8. **9:** It may at first appear like you don't have enough information to answer this question. If all you know is that the triangle is isosceles, then all you know is that two sides have equal length, which means the third side has a length of either 3 or 9. But if the third side were 3, then the lengths of two of the sides would not add up to greater than the length of the third side, because $3 + 3$ is not greater than 9:

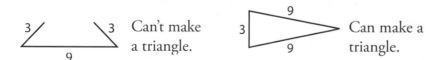

The length of the third side must be 9.

9. **(B):** There are two properties of a triangle at play here. The lengths of any two sides of a triangle must add up to greater than the length of the third side. Also, longer sides must be opposite larger angles. Answer choice (A). is out because side *AB* is opposite the largest angle, so side *AB* must have a length greater than 7. Answer choice (C). is out, because $4 + 7 = 11$, so the third side has to be less than 11. The only remaining possibility is choice (B), 10.

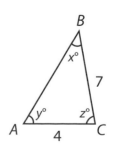

8

10. **30:** To find the area, you need a base and a height. If you can find the length of side *AB*, then *AB* can be the height and *AC* can be the base, because the two sides are perpendicular to each other.

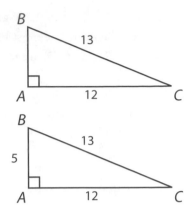

You can use the Pythagorean theorem to find the length of side *AB*: $(a)^2 + (12)^2 = (13)^2$. Thus: $a^2 + 144 = 169$. $a^2 = 25$. $a = 5$. Or you could recognize that the triangle is the Pythagorean triple 5–12–13.

Now that you know the length of side *AB*, you can find the area: $\frac{1}{2}(12) \times (5) = 30$.

11. **14.6:** To find the perimeter of triangle *ABC*, you need the lengths of all three sides. There is no immediately obvious way to find the length of side *BC*, so see what inferences you can make from the information the question gave.

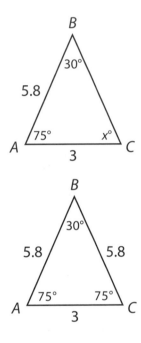

You know the degree measures of two of the angles in Triangle *ABC*, so you can find the degree measure of the third. Label the third angle *x*. You know that $30 + 75 + x = 180$. Solving for *x*, you find that $x = 75$.

Angles *BAC* and *ACB* are both 75, which means triangle *ABC* is an isosceles triangle. If those two angles are equal, you know that their opposite sides are also equal. Side *AB* has a length of 5.8, so you know that side *BC* also has a length of 5.8.

To find the perimeter, add up the lengths of the three sides: $5.8 + 5.8 + 3 = 14.6$.

12. $\sqrt{61}$: To find the length of the hypotenuse, you need the lengths of the other two sides. Then you can use the Pythagorean theorem to find the length of the hypotenuse. You can use the area formula to find the length of *AC*: Area $= \frac{1}{2}$ (base) $\times$ (height), and you know the area and the height. So $15 = \frac{1}{2}$ (base) $\times$ (5). When you solve this equation, you find that the base = 6.

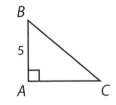

Now you can use the Pythagorean theorem: $(5)^2 + (6)^2 = c^2$. $25 + 36 = c^2$. $61 = c^2$. $\sqrt{61} = c$. Since 61 is not a perfect square, you know that *c* will be a decimal. Also, 61 is prime, so you cannot simplify $\sqrt{61}$ any further. (It will be a little less than $\sqrt{64} = 8$.)

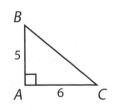

8

13. **10:** There is no immediately obvious way to find the length of side *HI*, so see what you can infer from the picture. You know two of the angles of Triangle *GHI*, so you can find the third. Label the third angle *x* and add the angles: 37 + 53 + *x* = 180. That means *x* = 90. So really your triangle looks like this:

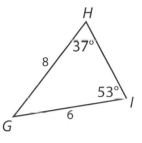

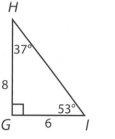

You should definitely redraw once you discover the triangle is a right triangle!

Now that you know triangle *GHI* is a right triangle, you can use the Pythagorean theorem to find the length of *HI*. Because *HI* is the hypotenuse: $(6)^2 + (8)^2 = c^2$. $36 + 64 = c^2$. Therefore, $100 = c^2$, so the length of *HI* is 10.

Alternatively, you could have recognized the Pythagorean triple. Triangle *GHI* is a 6–8–10 triangle.

14. **Triangle *DEF*:**

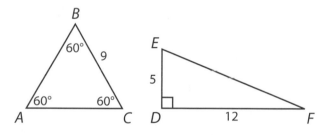

To determine which triangle has the greater perimeter, you need to know the side lengths of all three sides of both triangles. Begin with triangle *ABC*.

All three angles in triangle *ABC* are 60°. If all three angles are equal, that means all three sides are equal in this equilateral triangle. So every side of triangle *ABC* has a length of 9. That means the perimeter of *ABC* is 9 + 9 + 9 = 27.

Now look at triangle *DEF*. Triangle *DEF* is a right triangle, so you can use the Pythagorean theorem to find the length of side *EF*. Since side *EF* is the hypotenuse, $(5)^2 + (12)^2 = 25 + 144 = 169 = c^2$, which means that *c* = 13. That means the perimeter of *DEF* is 5 + 12 + 13 = 30. Alternatively, 5–12–13 is a Pythagorean triple.

Because 30 > 27, triangle *DEF* has a greater perimeter than triangle *ABC*.

8

15. **12:** Start by filling in everything you know about triangle *XYZ*.

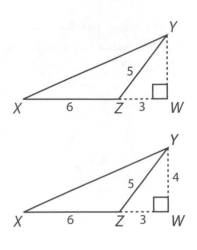

To find the area of triangle *XYZ*, you need a base and a height. If side *XZ* is a base, then *YW* can act as a height. You can find the length of *YW* because triangle *ZYW* is a right triangle, and you know the lengths of two of the sides. Since *YZ* is the hypotenuse, $(a)^2 + (3)^2 = (5)^2$ or $a^2 + 9 = 25$, so it follows that $a^2 = 16$ and $a = 4$.

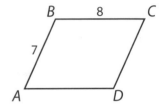

Or you could recognize the Pythagorean triple: *ZYW* is a 3–4–5 triangle. Now you know that the area of triangle *XYZ* is $\frac{1}{2}(b) \times (h) = \frac{1}{2}(6) \times (4) = 12$.

Drill Set 3

1. **30:** Opposite sides of a parallelogram are equal, so you know that side *CD* has a length of 7 and side *AD* has a length of 8. So the perimeter is $7 + 8 + 7 + 8 = 30$.

2. **40:**

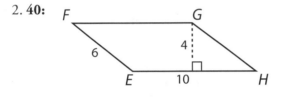

The area of a parallelogram is base × height. In this parallelogram, the base is 10 and the height is 4 (remember, base and height need to be perpendicular). So the area is $10 \times 4 = 40$.

3. **2:** First you can find the perimeter of parallelogram *ABCD*. Two sides have a length of 4, and two sides have a length of 5, so the perimeter is $2 \times (4 + 5) = 18$. That means parallelogram *EFGH* also has a perimeter of 18. Side *GH* also has a length of 7. You don't know the lengths of the other two sides, but you do know they have the same length, so for now call the length of each side *x*. The parallelogram now looks like this:

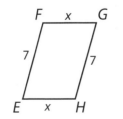

So you know that $7 + x + 7 + x = 18$ → $2x + 14 = 18$ → $2x = 4$ → $x = 2$
The length of side *EH* is 2.

4. **12:** One property that is true of any parallelogram is that the diagonal will split the parallelogram into two equal triangles. If triangle *ABC* has an area of 12, then triangle *ACD* must also have an area of 12.

5. **6:** Start by finding the area of rectangle *WXYZ*. The area of a rectangle is length × width, so the area of rectangle *WXYZ* is 3 × 4 = 12. So rectangle *OPQR* also has an area of 12. Likewise, you can use the same formula for the area of rectangle *OPQR*. Call the width 2 and the length *l*: $l \times 2 = 12 \rightarrow l = 6$. The length of side *PQ* is 6.

6. **12:** To find the area of rectangle *ABCD*, you need to know the length of side *AD* or side *BC*. In a rectangle, every internal angle is 90 degrees, so triangle *ABD* is actually a right triangle. That means you can use the Pythagorean theorem to find the length of side *AD*. Actually, this right triangle is one of the Pythagorean triples—a 3–4–5 triangle. The length of side *AD* is 3. That means the area of rectangle *ABCD* is 3 × 4 = 12.

7. **13:** You know the area of triangle *ABC* and the length of side *AB*. Because side *BC* is perpendicular to side *AB*, you can use those as the base and height of triangle *ABC*. So you know that $\frac{1}{2}(5) \times (BC)$ = 30. That means the length of side *BC* is 12.

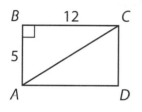

Now you can use the Pythagorean theorem to find the length of diagonal *AC*, which is the hypotenuse of right triangle *ABC*. You can also recognize that this is a Pythagorean triple—a 5–12–13 triangle. The length of diagonal *AC* is 13.

8. **4:** The first thing to notice in this problem is that you can find the length of side *CD*. Triangle *ACD* is a right triangle, and you know the lengths of two of the sides. You can either use the Pythagorean theorem or recognize that this is one of the Pythagorean triples—a 6–8–10 triangle. The length of side *CD* is 6. Now you can find the area of rectangle *ABCD*. Side *AD* is the length and side *CD* is the width. 8 × 6 = 48.

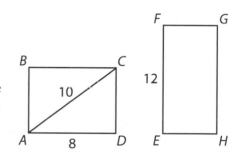

That means that the area of rectangle *EFGH* is also 48. You can use the area and the length of side *EF* to solve for the length of side *FG*: 12 × (*FG*) = 48. Thus, the length of side *FG* is 4.

9. **Length and width are 2 and 3:** In order to answer this question, begin by drawing a rectangle. In this rectangle, make one pair of equal sides have a length of *x*, and the other pair of equal sides has a length of *y*:

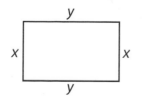

Using the lengths x and y, you know the perimeter of the rectangle is $2x + 2y$. So you know that: $2x + 2y = 10$. This can be simplified to $x + y = 5$.

You also know the area of the rectangle is $xy = 6$, so the area of the rectangle $= l \times w = 6$.

The easiest way to solve is to simply try values for x and y, aiming for a product of 6 and sum of 5. It shouldn't take long to find that 2 and 3 work. Or you could use substitution to solve for the values of the variables. In the first equation, you can isolate x: $x = 5 - y$.

Next, substitute $(5 - y)$ for x in the second equation:

$(5 - y)y = 6$
$5y - y^2 = 6$ This is a quadratic, so you need to get everything on one side.
$y^2 - 5y + 6 = 0$ Now factor the equation.
$(y - 3)(y - 2) = 0$

So $y = 2$ or 3.

When you plug in these values to solve for x, you find something a little unusual. When $y = 2$, $x = 3$. When $y = 3$, $x = 2$. What that means is that either the length is 2 and the width is 3, or the length is 3 and the width is 2. Both of these rectangles are identical, so you have the answer.

10. **30:** Triangle ABC and rectangle $JKLM$ have equal areas. What is the perimeter of rectangle $JKLM$?

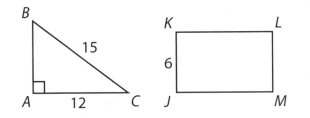

If you can find the length of side AB, then you can find the area of triangle ABC. You can use the Pythagorean theorem to find the length of side AB: $(12)^2 + (AB)^2 = (15)^2 \rightarrow 144 + AB^2 = 225 \rightarrow AB^2 = 81 \rightarrow AB = 9$. Notice that a 9–12–15 triangle is a 3–4–5 triangle with all the measurements tripled.

Now that you know AB, you can find the area of triangle ABC: $\frac{1}{2}(12) \times 9 = 54$.

That means that rectangle $JKLM$ also has an area of 54. You have one side of the rectangle, so you can solve for the other: $6 \times (JM) = 54$. Thus, the length of side JM is 9. That means that the perimeter is $2 \times (6 + 9) = 30$.

11. **20:** A square has four equal sides, so the area of a square is the length of one side squared. That means the lengths of the sides of the square are 5. If each of the four sides has a length of 5, then the perimeter is $4 \times 5 = 20$.

12. **16:** Start by drawing the shapes that the question describes:

The square has four equal sides, so that means that the perimeter is 4 times the length of one side. If you designate the length of the sides of the square s, then the perimeter is $4s = 32$. That means that s is 8. Now that you know the length of the sides, you can figure out the area of the square, which is 8^2. So the area of the square is 64.

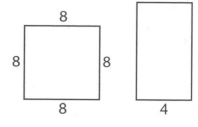

That means that the area of the rectangle is also 64. You know the length of the rectangle is 4, so you can solve for the width: $4 \times (\text{width}) = 64$. Thus, the width is 16.

13. **20.25π or $\dfrac{81\pi}{4}$:** You need to find a common link between the square and the circle, so that you can find the area of the circle. You know that the length of the sides of the square is 9. You can draw a new line in the figure that has the same length as the sides *and* is the diameter of the circle.

That means that the diameter of the circle is 9. If the diameter is 9, then the radius is 4.5, or $\dfrac{9}{2}$. That means the area of the circle is $\pi(4.5)^2$, or $\pi\left(\dfrac{9}{2}\right)^2$, which equals 20.25π, or $\dfrac{81\pi}{4}$.

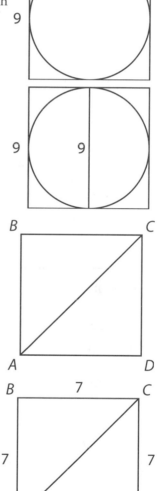

14. **$7\sqrt{2}$:** If the square has an area of 49, then $(\text{side})^2 = 49$. That means that the length of the sides of the square is 7.

Now you can use the Pythagorean theorem to find the length of diagonal AC, which is also the hypotenuse of triangle ACD: $7^2 + 7^2 = (AC)^2 \rightarrow 98 = (AC)^2 \rightarrow \sqrt{98} = AC$. But this can be simplified to $AC = \sqrt{2 \times 49} = \sqrt{2 \times 7 \times 7} = 7\sqrt{2}$.

Alternatively, you could remember that the diagonal of a square is always $s\sqrt{2}$, or $7\sqrt{2}$ in this case.

15. **4:** Triangle *ABC* is a right triangle, so you can find the length of hypotenuse *BC*. This is a 3–4–5 triangle, so the length of side *BC* is 5. That means the perimeter of triangle *ABC* is 3 + 4 + 5 = 12.

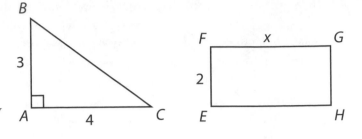

That means the perimeter of rectangle *EFGH* is also 12. That means that $2 \times (2 + x) = 12$, so $4 + 2x = 12 \rightarrow 2x = 8 \rightarrow x = 4$.

Drill Set 4

1. Draw a coordinate plane and plot the following points:

   1. (2, 3)   2. (−2, −1)   3. (−5, −6)   4. (4, −2.5)

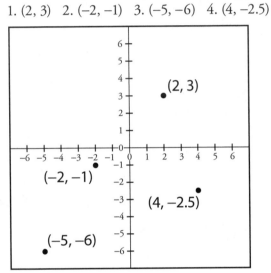

2. *A*: **(3, 0)**
   B: **(−3, 2)**
   C: **(1, −5)**
   D: **(0, −3)**

3. **−4:** On this line, the point with an x-coordinate of 3 is the point $(3, -4)$. The y-coordinate of the point is −4. This is easiest to see by simply tracing your finger from the x-intercept of 3 directly down to the line, then briefly left to the y-axis. Alternatively, you can use the given points to determine the slope, which is −1, and then use that, along with the y-intercept of −1, to create the equation of the line: $y = -x - 1$. Plug in 3 for x, and $y = -4$:

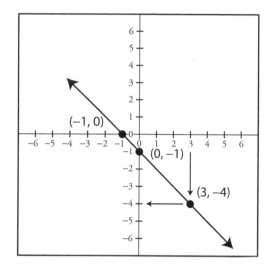

4. **−2:** Trace your finger from the y-intercept of −4 directly left to the line, then directly up to the x-axis. The x-intercept is −2:

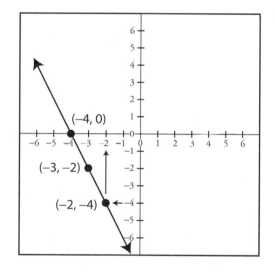

5. **Yes:** For the point $(3, -2)$ to lie on the line $y = 2x - 8$, y needs to equal −2 when you plug in 3 for x:

$$y = 2(3) - 8$$
$$y = 6 - 8 = -2$$

Thus, y does equal −2 when x equals 3, so the point does lie on the line.

6. **No:** For the point $(-3, 0)$ to lie on the curve $y = x^2 - 3$, y needs to equal 0 when you plug in -3 for x:

$$y = (-3)^2 - 3$$
$$y = 9 - 3 = 6$$

Thus, y does not equal 0 when x equals -3, so the point does not lie on the curve.

7. **14:** To find the y-coordinate, you need to plug in 3 for x and solve for y:

$$y = 4(3) + 2$$
$$y = 12 + 2 = 14$$

The y-coordinate is 14. The point is $(3, 14)$.

8. **−7:** The equation of the line is already in $y = mx + b$ form, and b stands for the y-intercept, so you just need to look at the equation to find the y-intercept. The equation is $y = -2x - 7$. That means the y-intercept is -7. The point is $(0, -7)$.

9. The slope (m) is 1/3, so the line slopes gently up to the right, rising only 1 unit for every 3 units of run.

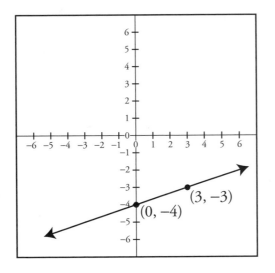

The y-intercept (b) is -4, so the line crosses the y-axis at $(0, -4)$.

MANHATTAN
PREP

8

10. Before you can graph the line, put the equation into $y = mx + b$ form. Next, multiply both sides by 2.

$y = -x + 2$

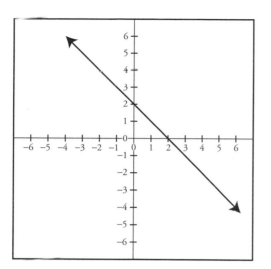

The slope (m) is −1, so the line drops to the right, falling 1 unit for every unit of run.

The y-intercept is 2, so the line crosses the y-axis at (0, 2).

8

Chapter 9
of Geometry

Geometry Practice Question Sets

In This Chapter...

Easy Practice Question Set

1.

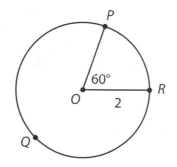

Point *O* is the center of the circle.

Quantity A	Quantity B
The length of arc *PQR*	3π

2. If a triangle has sides measuring 5 inches and 12 inches, which of the following could <u>not</u> be the measure of the third side?

   (A)   7.5 inches
   (B)   10 inches
   (C) 12.5 inches
   (D)   15 inches
   (E) 17.5 inches

3.

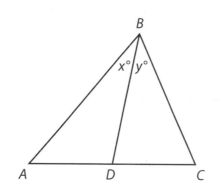

$AD = DC$

Quantity A	Quantity B
x	*y*

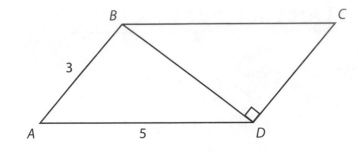

4. The area of parallelogram *ABCD* equals

    (A) 6
    (B) 7.5
    (C) $5\sqrt{3}$
    (D) 12
    (E) 15

5.

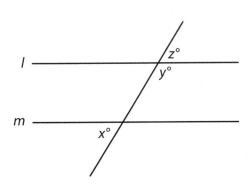

Lines *l* and *m* are parallel.

Quantity A	**Quantity B**
$y - z$	x

6. What is the *x*-intercept of the line $2x + 5y = 7$?

    (A) 1
    (B) 1.4
    (C) 2
    (D) 3
    (E) 3.5

7. Swimming Pool A has a perimeter of 100 meters. Swimming Pool B has a perimeter of 80 meters. Both swimming pools are rectangular.

Quantity A	**Quantity B**
The area of Swimming Pool A, in square meters	The area of Swimming Pool B, in square meters

8.

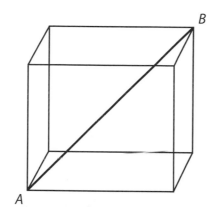

The cube has edges of length 10.

Quantity A	**Quantity B**
The length of the diagonal from point A to point B	17

9.

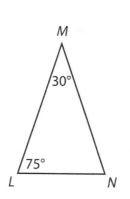

Quantity A	**Quantity B**
The length of LM	The length of MN

10. In the xy-plane, the equation of line k is $4x + 5y = 3$.

Quantity A	**Quantity B**
The x-intercept of line k	The y-intercept of line k

9

11.

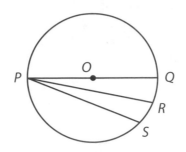

PQ is a diameter of the circle above.

Quantity A	**Quantity B**
The length of PR	The average (arithmetic mean) of the lengths of PQ and PS

12.

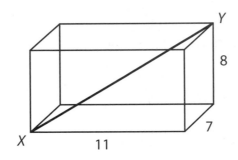

For the rectangular solid above, the square of the length of the diagonal XY is what?

13.

In the figure above, the diameter of the circle is 12.

Quantity A	**Quantity B**
The area of rectangle PQRS	80

MANHATTAN
PREP

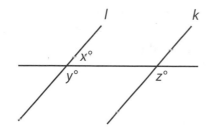

14. In the figure above, lines *l* and *k* are parallel. If $y - x = 30$, what is *z*?

    (A)   60

    (B)   75

    (C)   90

    (D) 105

    (E) 120

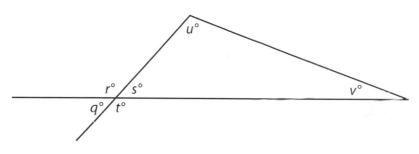

15. In the figure above, having values for which of the following expressions individually would be sufficient to solve for the value of *r*?

    Indicate <u>all</u> such values.

    A *q*

    B *s*

    C *t*

    D *u*

    E *v*

    F $s + u$

    G $u + v$

9

16. If two lines intersect such that one of the angles formed at the intersection measures 20°, which of the following is the closest approximation of the <u>product</u> of the degree measures of <u>all four</u> angles formed at the intersection?

    (A) 1×10^7

    (B) 2×10^7

    (C) 4×10^7

    (D) 2×10^8

    (E) 4×10^8

17.

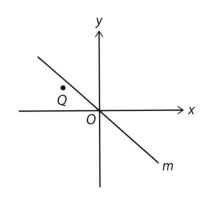

Quantity A	**Quantity B**
The slope of line *m*	The slope of line *n*

18.

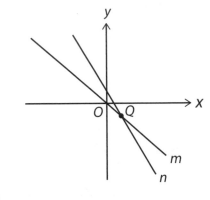

Point *Q* lies at (−3, 2).

Quantity A	**Quantity B**
The slope of line *m*	−1

19. Line *k* in the *xy*-plane goes through the point (1, 1) and has a negative slope. Which of the following points could lie on line *k*?

    Indicate all such points.

    A (1, 2)
    B (2, 0)
    C (−2, 0)
    D (−2, 2)

20.

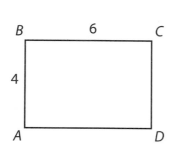
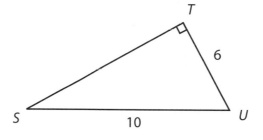

Quantity A	**Quantity B**
The area of rectangle *ABCD*	The area of Triangle *STU*

9

Geometry: Easy Practice Question Solutions

1. (A): To find the length of arc *PQR*, you first need to calculate the circumference of the circle. This is found by the equation $C = \pi d = 2\pi r$. Because *O* is the center of the circle, you can use *OR* = 2 as the radius. Therefore, $C = 2\pi(2) = 4\pi$. Because $\frac{1}{6}$ of the circle is *not* included in arc *PQR* (60° is $\frac{1}{6}$ of 360°), the remaining $\frac{5}{6}$ of the circumference represents the length of arc *PQR*. Hence, arc $PQR = \frac{5}{6}(4\pi) = \frac{20\pi}{6} = \frac{10\pi}{3}$. Or, put simply:

Quantity A	**Quantity B**
$\frac{10}{3}\pi$	3π

Because $\frac{10}{3} > 3$, **Quantity A is greater**.

2. (E): Any side *x* of a triangle must be *greater* than the difference between the lengths of the two other sides, and *less* than the sum of the two other sides. In this case, the third side must be between (12 − 5) = 7 inches, and (12 + 5) = 17 inches. Therefore, 7 < *x* < 17. Only 17.5 inches is outside this range.

3. (D): Even though line segments *AD* and *DC* have equal lengths, the relationship between angle measures *x* and *y* is indeterminate. If *BD* is perpendicular to *AC*, as shown in the figure to the left (below), then *x* = *y*. However, if point *B* is skewed to one side, then the angle on that side becomes larger than the other. For example, in the figure to the right (below), *x* > *y*:

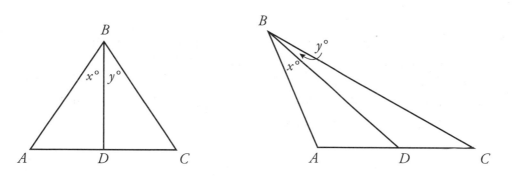

You cannot infer anything from the appearance of the drawing, so **the relationship cannot be determined from the information given**.

4. (D): Parallelogram *ABCD* is comprised of two congruent (identical) right triangles, *ABD* and *CBD*. The length of diagonal *BD* is 4, as can be determined from the Pythagorean theorem or the 3–4–5 triangle rule. Thus, the area of each of the right triangles is $\frac{1}{2} \times 3 \times 4 = 6$, and the area of *ABCD* is 12.

9

5. **(D):** In the figure, $x = z$ (alternate exterior angles of a transversal) and $y + z = 180$ (supplementary angles), which implies $y + x = 180$. So in terms of x, $z = x$ and $y = 180 - x$. Write Quantity A in terms of x:

Quantity A	**Quantity B**
$y - z = (180 - x) - x$	x
$= \mathbf{180 - 2x}$	

If $x = 5$, Quantity A is $170 > 5$. If $x = 80$, Quantity A is $20 < 80$.

Depending on the value of x, either $180 - 2x$ or x may be greater, or the two quantities may be equal. **The relationship cannot be determined from the information given.** Even though angle x appears to be acute, you do not know that it must be acute.

6. **(E):** The x-intercept of a line is the value of x at which the line crosses the x-axis. When a line crosses the x-axis, the value of y equals 0. Thus, the x-intercept can be determined by setting y equal to 0 in the equation for the line: $2x + 0 = 7$, so $x = 3.5$.

7. **(D):** Even though both swimming pools are rectangular and Swimming Pool A has a larger perimeter, it is possible for Swimming Pool B to cover a larger area or the same area as Swimming Pool A. For example, Swimming Pool A could have a length of 40 meters and a width of 10 meters (Perimeter = $2 \times$ length $+ 2 \times$ width for rectangles). This would give Swimming Pool A an area of $40 \times 10 = 400$ square meters. If Swimming Pool B is square, its area would be maximized at $\left(\dfrac{80}{4}\right)^2 = 20^2 = 400$, equal to that of Swimming Pool A. If instead Swimming Pool B had a length of 30 meters and a width of 10 meters, its area would equal $30 \times 10 = 300$ square meters. It is also possible to construct examples in which Swimming Pool A has a smaller area than Pool B. Thus, **the relationship cannot be determined from the information given.**

8. **(A):** The formula for the length of a diagonal across opposite ends of a rectangular solid is as follows: $d^2 = l^2 + w^2 + h^2$, where l, w, and h are the length, width, and height of the rectangular solid. Since $l = w = h$ for a square, you can simplify this to: $d^2 = 3l^2$. Since $l = 10$, $d^2 = 3(10)^2$, and $d = 10\sqrt{3}$. Using the GRE on-screen calculator, you can determine that $\sqrt{3}$ is slightly larger than 1.7, so d is slightly larger than 17. Thus, **Quantity A is greater.**

9. **(C):** Because the interior angles of a triangle must sum to $180°$, angle LNM must equal $180 - 75 - 30 = 75$. Therefore, triangle LMN is an isosceles triangle, and sides LM and MN must be equal length. Therefore, **the two quantities are equal.**

10. **(A):** To find the x-intercept, set $y = 0$ and solve for x. Similarly, to find the y-intercept, set $x = 0$ and solve for y.

x-intercept:	$4x + 5(0) = 3$	$4x = 3$	$x = \dfrac{3}{4} = 0.75$
y-intercept:	$4(0) + 5y = 3$	$5y = 3$	$y = \dfrac{3}{5} = 0.60$

Therefore, **Quantity A is greater.**

9

11. **(D):** Notice that a diameter (such as *PQ* in the diagram) is the largest chord that can be drawn through a circle. The farther a chord passes from the center, the smaller the chord will be. Therefore, *PQ* > *PR* > *PS*. The question asks you to compare the length of *PR*, the middle-length chord, to the average of *PQ* and *PS*:

$$\text{Is } PR > \frac{PQ + PS}{2} \, ?$$

Multiplying by 2, you get, is 2*PR* > *PQ* + *PS*?

By moving *PR* and *PS* around, you can see that, in some cases, 2*PR* will be larger; in others, *PQ* + *PS* will be larger:

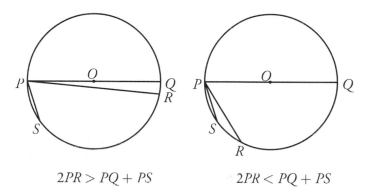

$$2PR > PQ + PS \qquad\qquad 2PR < PQ + PS$$

Therefore, **the relationship cannot be determined from the information given**.

12. **234:** To calculate the diagonal of a rectangular solid, you can simply take the sum of the squares of the length, width, and height, and take the square root. (This is the mathematical equivalent of using the Pythagorean theorem twice in succession.) For this problem, you need only report the square of the length, so you do not need to find the square root of the sum of the squared sides:

$$(xy)^2 = 11^2 + 7^2 + 8^2 = 121 + 49 + 64 = 234$$

13. **(B):** Given that the diameter of the circle is 12, the area of the circle is given by $\pi r^2 = \pi\left(\dfrac{d}{2}\right)^2 = \pi\left(\dfrac{12}{2}\right)^2 = 36\pi$. The inscribed rectangle *PQRS* must be smaller than that. The question is, what are the limitations on its size?

To picture the smallest possible rectangle, envision one extremely short and wide, as in the figure at left, on the next page. This rectangle would have a width approaching that of the circle's diameter (12), but a height approaching 0. Thus, the area would approach 0.

To picture the largest possible rectangle, envision a perfect square. As in the figure at right below, the diagonal *PR* = 12, which is also a diameter of the circle. This diameter cuts the square into two 45–45–90 triangles, which have sides in the proportion $1 : 1 : \sqrt{2}$. Therefore, the side of the square would equal

9

$\frac{12}{\sqrt{2}} = 6\sqrt{2}$, and the area would equal $\left(6\sqrt{2}\right)^2 = 72$, which is less than Quantity B (80). Therefore, the rectangle will always have an area smaller than Quantity B. Thus, **Quantity B is greater**.

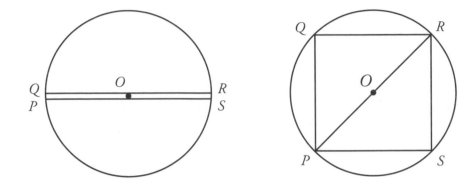

14. **(D):** Because l and k are parallel, the horizonal line creates a transversal. As a result, $y = z$. In addition, $x + y = 180$, because x and y are supplementary angles. The question stem tells you that $y - x = 30$. If you add these two equations together, you get $2y = 210$, or $y = 105$. Therefore, $z = 105$.

15. **(A), (B), (C), and (G):** Because s, u, and v are the interior angles of a triangle, $s + u + v = 180$. Also, since r and s are supplementary angles, $r + s = 180$. Therefore, $s + u + v = r + s$, which implies that $u + v = r$. So knowing the value of $u + v$ would enable you to solve for r. Thus, choice (G) is correct. Knowing u or v individually would not enable you to solve for r, nor would knowing the sum $s + u$. (That sum would enable you to solve for v, which you have already established is not sufficient to solve for r.)

As previously stated, $r + s = 180$, so knowing s would enable you to solve for r. Thus, choice (C) is correct.

Finally, q and s are opposite angles, as are r and t, so $q = s$ and $r = t$. Thus, knowing t gives you r directly, and knowing q gives you s directly, which were already demonstrated to be sufficient. Thus, choices (A) and (B) are correct.

16. **(A):** Because one of the angles formed equals 20°, the other angles must measure 20°, 160°, and 160° (see diagram):

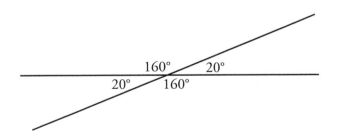

Therefore, the product of all four degree measures $= (20)^2(160)^2 = 400 \times 25{,}600 = 10{,}240{,}000$. This is very close to 10,000,000, or 1×10^7.

17. **(A):** Slope is defined as $\dfrac{\text{change in } y}{\text{change in } x}$, or $\dfrac{\text{rise}}{\text{run}}$. In the given diagram, both lines have a negative slope, but for any given change in x, the negative change in y is larger for line n than for line m. (In other words, line n is "falling" faster than line m). Therefore, the *absolute value* of the slope of line n is larger than that of line m, but since *both slopes are negative*, the slope of line m is the larger quantity. In other words, the slope of m is less negative than the slope of n. Therefore, **Quantity A is greater**.

18. **(D):** Because the point Q lies at $(-3, 2)$, the slope of a line containing both Q and the origin (O) has a slope of $-\dfrac{2}{3}$. Line m is steeper than that, with a negative slope. Therefore, the slope of line m is $< -\dfrac{2}{3}$.

It is possible for the slope to be $-\dfrac{3}{4}$, -1, or -2, for example. Therefore, **the relationship cannot be determined from the information given**.

19. **(B) and (D):** The easiest way to solve this problem is to draw the xy-plane with each of the points in the answer choices plotted:

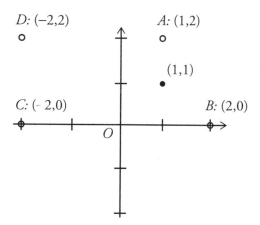

Drawing a line between $(1, 1)$ and choice (A) would produce a vertical line (infinite or undefined slope).

Drawing a line between $(1, 1)$ and choice (B) would produce a line with negative slope (-1).

Drawing a line between $(1, 1)$ and choice (C) would produce a line with positive slope $\left(\dfrac{1}{3}\right)$.

Drawing a line between $(1, 1)$ and choice (D) would produce a line with negative slope $\left(-\dfrac{1}{3}\right)$.

Therefore, choices (B) and (D) satisfy the conditions in the problem.

20. **(C):** The formula for the area of rectangle $ABCD = l \times w = 6 \times 4 = 24$. To figure out the area of triangle STU, use the Pythagorean theorem to solve for ST (the base of the triangle): $6^2 + ST^2 = 10^2$. Therefore, $ST^2 = 64$ and $ST = 8$. Alternatively, you could recognize that triangle STU is a 6–8–10 triangle.

The area of a triangle is given by the formula $\dfrac{1}{2}bh$, which in this case equals $\dfrac{1}{2}(8)(6) = 24$.

Therefore, **the two quantities are equal**.

9

Medium Practice Question Set

1. In the coordinate plane, for which of the following values of x would the graph of the equation $y = x^3 - x^2 - 6x$ touch the x axis?

    (A) 2
    (B) −3
    (C) −2
    (D) 1
    (E) 6

2. Points P, Q, and R lie in the coordinate plane. If $P = (1, 5)$, $Q = (1, 1)$, and $R = (7, y)$, how many different integer values for y could be chosen to form Triangle PQR, such that none of the angles in Triangle PQR is greater than 90°?

    (A) 0
    (B) 3
    (C) 5
    (D) 7
    (E) It cannot be determined from the information given.

3.

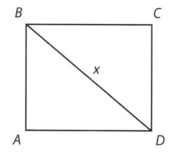

Polygon $ABCD$ is a square.

<table>
<tr><td><u>Quantity A</u></td><td><u>Quantity B</u></td></tr>
<tr><td>0.6x</td><td>The length of side CD</td></tr>
</table>

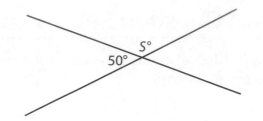

4. In the figure above, $S = xy$, where x and y are positive integers. Which of the following could be the value of x?

    Indicate <u>all</u> such values.

    A 26
    B 25
    C 10
    D 5
    E 4
    F 0

5.   Right triangle *PRS* has sides of length 6, 8, and x.

    Quantity A   **Quantity B**
         x 10

6.

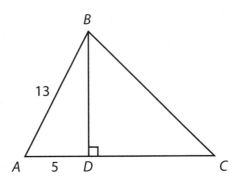

    In the figure above, $\angle CBD = \angle BCD$. What is the area of triangle *ABC*?

9

MANHATTAN
PREP

7.

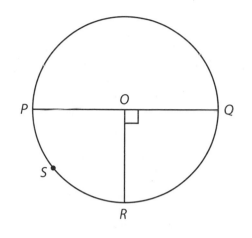

PQ is a diameter of the circle centered at *O*. If the area of sector *RSPO* equals 4π, then the circumference of the circle is how many times π?

8.

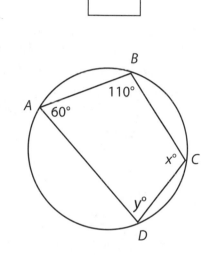

Quadrilateral *ABCD* is inscribed in a circle. What is *x* − *y*?

9.

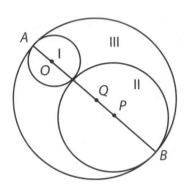

Circles I, II, and III are mutually tangent with centers O, P, and Q, respectively. Points O, P, and Q lie on line segment AB.

<table>
<tr><th>Quantity A</th><th>Quantity B</th></tr>
<tr><td>The sum of the circumferences of circles I and II</td><td>The circumference of circle III</td></tr>
</table>

10. A gardener plants two rectangular gardens in separate regions on her property. The first garden has an area of 600 square feet and a length of 40 feet. If the second garden has a width twice that of the first garden, but only half the area, what is the ratio of the perimeter of the first garden to that of the second garden?

$$\frac{\boxed{}}{\boxed{}}$$

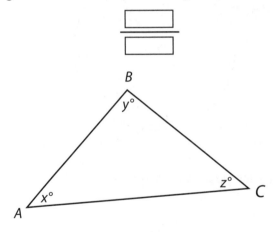

11. Triangle ABC's longest side is length 10. If $x \neq y \neq z$ and each side has an integer length, which of the following could be the length of its shortest side?

   Indicate all such lengths.

   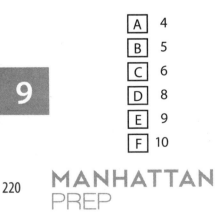

   [A] 4
   [B] 5
   [C] 6
   [D] 8
   [E] 9
   [F] 10

12.

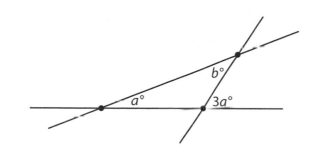

Quantity A	**Quantity B**
a	b

13. A circular garden is surrounded by a fence (the width of the fence is negligible) along its boundary. If the number of meters in length of the fence is half the number of square meters in the area of the garden, what is the radius of the circular garden?

    (A)   1

    (B)   2

    (C)   4

    (D)   8

    (E) 16

14.

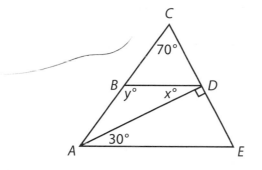

If $AB = BD$, then what is the value of $\dfrac{x}{y}$?

15. What is the perimeter, in inches, of a rectangular sandbox 5 feet long that has twice the area of a rectangular sandbox 20 feet long and 5 feet wide?

    (A)   600

    (B)   800

    (C)   960

    (D) 1,080

    (E) 1,200

9

16. In any square, the relationship between the area A and the perimeter P is $A = nP^2$, where n is a constant. What is the value of n^2?

    (A) $\dfrac{1}{4}$

    (B) $\dfrac{1}{8}$

    (C) $\dfrac{1}{32}$

    (D) $\dfrac{1}{64}$

    (E) $\dfrac{1}{256}$

17. P, Q, and R are each rectangles. The length and width of rectangle P are 30 percent less and 20 percent greater, respectively, than the length and width of rectangle R. The length and width of rectangle Q are 40 percent greater and 40 percent less, respectively, than the length and width of rectangle R.

<table>
<tr><td>Quantity A</td><td>Quantity B</td></tr>
<tr><td>The area of rectangle P</td><td>The area of rectangle Q</td></tr>
</table>

18.

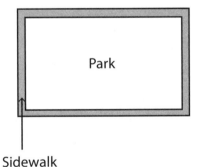

Sidewalk

The figure above represents a rectangular park with a sidewalk surrounding it. The park is 150 feet long and 90 feet wide, not including the sidewalk. The sidewalk is 5 feet wide all the way around. The area of the sidewalk alone is how many square feet?

    [   ] square feet

19.

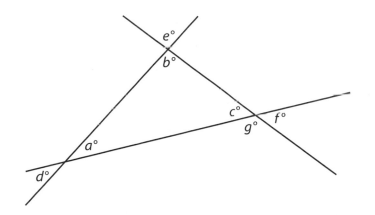

In the figure above, having values for which of the following expressions would be sufficient to solve for the value of c?

Indicate all such values.

A $\quad a$

B $\quad b$

C $\quad f$

D $\quad a+b$

E $\quad d+e$

F $\quad d+f$

G $\quad g$

20.

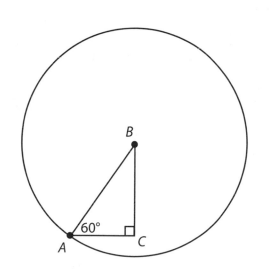

The circumference of the circle centered at point B is 12π.

Quantity A

14

Quantity B

The perimeter of triangle ABC

Geometry: Medium Practice Question Solutions

1. (C): In the coordinate plane, a line crosses the x-axis at values of x that return a y value of 0. These points are known as the "roots" of the equation. To find the roots of the equation $y = x^3 - x^2 - 6x$, set $y = 0$ and factor the right side of the equation as follows:

$$0 = x^3 - x^2 - 6x$$
$$0 = x(x^2 - x - 6)$$
$$0 = x(x + 2)(x - 3)$$

Hence, $y = 0$ when $x = 0, -2,$ or 3. Only choice (C) matches one of these roots.

2. (C): An obtuse angle is an angle with degree measure higher than 90°. As the following diagram shows, if y is greater than 5 or less than 1, it will cause triangle PQR to have an obtuse angle. Therefore, y must be an integer between 1 and 5, inclusive:

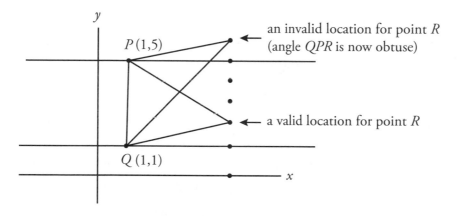

3. (B): The ratio of the length of a side of a square to the length of its diagonal (labeled x in this diagram) is $1 : \sqrt{2}$, because the diagonal divides the square into two right isosceles (45–45–90) triangles. You can find the length of a side of the square by dividing x by $\sqrt{2}$. Since $\sqrt{2}$ is roughly equal to 1.4 (or $\frac{7}{5}$), side BD equals approximately $\frac{x}{7/5}$, or $\frac{5x}{7}$. This equals approximately 0.7x. Therefore, **Quantity B is greater**.

4. (A), (C), and (D): Since 5° and 50° are supplementary, $S = 180 - 50 = 30$. Since $S = xy$, it must be true that $xy = 130$.

From there, you need to determine which integers could multiply to produce 130. You can break 130 down into the prime factors $2 \times 5 \times 13$, so any factor of 130 must be composed of *only some subset* of these prime factors. The answer choices 25 and 4 are not composed strictly of 2, 5, and 13. Furthermore, 0 cannot be possible, because if x were equal to 0, S would have to equal 0.

9

5. **(D):** The trap in this problem is the common (but faulty) assumption that 6 and 8 are the lengths of the two perpendicular sides of a right triangle, because 6–8–10 triangles are common on the GRE.

If that were the case, the Pythagorean theorem or the 3–4–5 triangle rule could be used to determine that the length x of the hypotenuse equals 10: $6^2 + 8^2 = 10^2$. However, it is also possible that the side with length 8 is the hypotenuse of the triangle. In that case: $6^2 + x^2 = 8^2$, and $x = \sqrt{28} = 2\sqrt{7} \neq 10$.

6. **102:** The right triangle on the left (triangle ABD) is a 5–12–13 triangle, which is one of the common right triangles with integer side lengths. (Note that you could also use the Pythagorean theorem to determine that the length of BD equals 12: $5^2 + 12^2 = 13^2$.) BD is the height of triangle ABC.

Because $\angle CBD = \angle BCD$, triangle BCD is isosceles, and the length of CD must also equal 12. Thus, the base of triangle ABC has length 5 + 12 = 17, and its area is given by $\frac{1}{2}bh = \frac{1}{2}(17)(12) = 17 \times 6 = 102$.

7. **8:** Because angle ROQ is a right angle and POQ is a straight line, angle POR must also be a right angle. Angle POR is the central angle of sector $RSPO$. Therefore, the area of sector $RSPO$ must be 1/4 of the entire circle (90° is one-fourth of 360°). The area of the entire circle is found as follows: $4 \times 4\pi = 16\pi$. Using the area formula for a circle, you obtain $\pi r^2 = 16\pi$, so $r = \sqrt{16} = 4$. Finally, the circumference of the circle is found from the formula $c = 2\pi r = 8\pi$. The circumference of the circle is 8 times π.

8. **50°:** When a quadrilateral is inscribed in a circle, opposite angles must add up to 180°. This is because all angles of such a quadrilateral are inscribed angles of a circle. For example, angle ADC intercepts arc ABC, and angle ABC intercepts arc ADC. The two arcs constitute the entire circle. Thus, the sum of the arcs intercepted by these angles is a whole circle, or 360, and the angles must sum to $\frac{1}{2}(360°) = 180°$. (This follows from the rule that the measure of an inscribed angle of a circle is one-half the measure of the corresponding central angle.) This gives $x = 180 - 60 = 120$ and $y = 180 - 110 = 70$. Combining, $x - y = 120 - 70 = 50$.

9. **(C):** Because O, P, and Q all lie on line segment AB, the diameter of circle I (call it D_I) plus the diameter of circle II (D_{II}) must equal the diameter of circle III (D_{III}): $D_I + D_{II} = D_{III}$. Because the circumference of a circle equals the diameter times π (i.e., $c = \pi d$), you can write $\pi(D_I + D_{II}) = \pi D_{III}$, or (letting C denote circumference), $(C_I + C_{II}) = C_{III}$. Therefore, **the two quantities are equal**.

10. $\frac{110}{80}$ **(or any equivalent):** According to the problem, the first garden has an area of 600 square feet and a length of 40 feet. Therefore, the width of the garden is $\frac{600}{40} = 15$ feet. The second garden has a width twice that amount (30 feet), and an area only half that of the first garden ($\frac{1}{2}$ of 600 square feet = 300 square feet). Therefore, the length of the second garden is $\frac{300}{30} = 10$ feet.

The perimeter of the first garden is 2 × length + 2 × width = 2(40) + 2(15) = 110.

The perimeter of the second garden is 2 × length + 2 × width = 2(10) + 2(30) = 80.

9

MANHATTAN
PREP

Thus, the correct ratio is $\dfrac{110}{80}$ (or the mathematical equivalent).

11. **(A)**, **(B)**, **(C)**, and **(D)**: According to the problem, the longest side of the triangle is 10, each side has an integer length, and none of the angles are equal. Since none of the angles are equal, none of the sides can be equal. Therefore, choice (F) can be eliminated—if the shortest side were 10, then all three sides would have to equal 10, yielding an equilateral triangle (all angles equal).

Similarly, if the shortest side were length 9, then the third side would have to equal 9 or 10. This would yield an isosceles triangle, and two of the angles would have to be equal. Choice (E) can thus be eliminated.

All of the other choices are possible. For example, the sides could be 4–7–10 (satisfying choice (A)), 5–7–10 (satisfying choice (B)), 6–7–10 (satisfying choice (C)), or 8–9–10 (satisfying choice (D)).

12. **(B)**: Because $3a$ is an exterior angle to the triangle enclosed by the three lines in the diagram, $3a$ must equal $a + b$. This is easiest to see by adding a label to the third angle in the triangle:

$a + b + c = 180$ (interior angles of a triangle)
$c + 3a = 180$ (supplementary angles)

Therefore, $a + b + c = c + 3a$, and $a + b = 3a$. Thus, $b = 2a$, and since angles must have a positive value, $b > a$. Thus, **Quantity B is greater**.

13. **(C)**: If a circular garden is surrounded by a fence of negligible width, the fence will have a length equal to the circumference of the garden. Thus, the length of the fence is given by $C = 2\pi r$. The area of the garden is given by the formula for the area of a circle, $A = \pi r^2$. Finally, the problem tells you that the length of the fence is half the area of the garden, so you can write the equation as:

$$C = \left(\frac{1}{2}\right)(A)$$
$$2\pi r = \frac{1}{2}\pi r^2$$
$$4\pi r = \pi r^2$$
$$4r = r^2$$
$$0 = r^2 - 4r$$
$$0 = r(r - 4)$$
$$r = 0 \text{ and } r = 4$$

9

The garden cannot have a 0 radius, so the radius of the garden must be 4. The correct answer is choice (C).

14. $\dfrac{20}{140}$ **(or any equivalent):** According to the problem, $AB = BD$. Therefore, triangle ABD is an isosceles triangle, and angle BAD is equal to x. Additionally, since you know angle $ADE = 90$ and angle $DAE = 30$, you can determine that angle $AED = 180 - 90 - 30 = 60$ (since these three angles form the triangle ADE). You can update the diagram as follows:

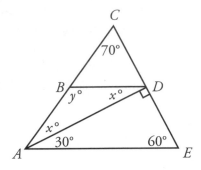

The angles of the large triangle, ACE, must sum to 180. Therefore, $70 + 60 + 30 + x = 180$, so $x = 20$. Since y, x, and x must sum to 180 (they form the angles of triangle ABD), $y = 180 - 2x$, so $y = 140$.

Thus, the correct ratio is $\dfrac{20}{140}$ (or the mathematical equivalent).

15. **(D):** If the sandbox with a length of 5 feet has twice the area of the other sandbox (which has an area of $20 \times 5 = 100$ square feet), it must have an area of 200 square feet. Therefore, its width must equal $\dfrac{200}{5} = 40$ feet. Since the formula for the perimeter of a rectangle is $2l + 2w$, the perimeter is $2(5) + 2(40) = 10 + 80 = 90$ feet. Converting to inches, the perimeter is $90 \times 12 = 1{,}080$ inches.

16. **(E):** The area of a square is given by the formula $A = s^2$, where s is the length of the square's side. The perimeter is given by $P = 4s$. Plugging these values into the equation given in the question, you can solve for n:

$$(s^2) = n \times (4s)^2$$
$$s^2 = 16s^2 n$$
$$n = \frac{s^2}{16s^2} = \frac{1}{16}$$

Thus, $n^2 = \left(\dfrac{1}{16}\right)^2 = \dfrac{1}{256}$.

17. **(C):** In this question you are asked to compare the area of rectangle P with that of rectangle Q. Since the information given is the relative size of the length and width of rectangles P and Q with respect to

MANHATTAN
PREP

those of rectangle R, you should try to evaluate the relative areas using rectangle R's dimensions as the starting point.

If you assign x to the length of rectangle R, and y to its width, you get an area for rectangle R of xy. Because the length and width of rectangle P are 30 percent less and 20 percent greater, respectively, than those of rectangle R, then the length and width of rectangle P equal $(1 - 0.3)x = 0.7x$ and $(1 + 0.2)y = 1.2y$. Thus, the area of rectangle P is $(0.7x)(1.2y) = 0.84xy$.

Similarly, the length and width of rectangle Q are 40 percent greater and 40 percent less, respectively, than those of rectangle R, so the length and width of rectangle Q equal $(1 + 0.4)x = 1.4x$ and $(1 - 0.4)y = 0.6y$. Thus, the area of rectangle Q is $(1.4x)(0.6y) = 0.84xy$.

Thus, rectangles P and Q have equal area. Therefore, **the two quantities are equal**.

18. **2,500:** The region represented by the smaller rectangle is the park. The sidewalk is the shaded region all around it. Because the sidewalk is 5 feet wide, the larger rectangle (including the sidewalk) is 10 feet longer and wider than the park itself. Therefore, the larger rectangle, which includes both the sidewalk and the park, is 160 feet long and 100 feet wide. The area covered by the sidewalk alone can be found by subtracting the area of the larger rectangle from that of the smaller rectangle:

> Larger rectangle area: $160 \times 100 = 16,000$
> Smaller rectangle area: $150 \times 90 = 13,500$

The sidewalk therefore covers a total area of $16,000 - 13,500 = 2,500$.

19. **(C), (D), (E), and (G):** Because a, b, and c are the interior angles of a triangle, $a + b + c = 180$. Therefore, knowing the value of $a + b$ would enable you to solve for c. Thus, choice (D) is correct. Similarly, c and g are supplementary angles, so $c + g = 180$. Knowing g would enable you to solve for c, so choice (G) is correct.

In addition, because a and d are opposite angles, as are b and e, and as are c and f, you know that $a = d$, $b = e$, and $c = f$. Thus, if $a + b$ is sufficient to solve for c, so is $d + e$. Thus, choice (E) is correct. Finally, directly because $c = f$, choice (C) is correct.

20. **(B):** Plugging the circumference of the circle into the formula $C = 2\pi r$, you get $(12\pi) = 2\pi r$, so $r = 6$ and $AB = 6$.

Triangle ABC is a 30–60–90 triangle, so the proportions of the sides must be $1 : \sqrt{3} : 2$. Therefore: $AC = (6) \times \dfrac{1}{2} = 3$ and $BC = (6) \times \dfrac{\sqrt{3}}{2} = 3\sqrt{3}$. The perimeter of triangle ABC is therefore:

$6 + 3 + 3\sqrt{3} = 9 + 3\sqrt{3}$. Since $\sqrt{3} \approx 1.7$, you can estimate the perimeter to be $9 + 3(1.7) = 14.1$, which is larger than 14. (Note that $\sqrt{3}$ is actually larger than 1.7, so the perimeter will actually be slightly larger than 14.1.) This would be a good problem on which to use the GRE on-screen calculator.

9

Hard Practice Question Set

CAUTION: These problems are *very difficult*—likely more difficult than many of the problems you will see on the GRE. Consider these "Challenge Problems." Have fun!

1.

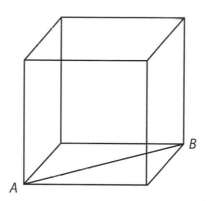

In the cube above, the length of line segment *AB* is 8. The surface area of the cube equals what?

2.

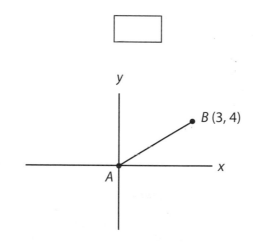

In the coordinate plane above, point *C* is not displayed. If the length of line segment *BC* is *twice* the length of line segment *AB*, which of the following could *not* be the coordinates of point *C*?

(A) (−5, −2)

(B) (9, 12)

(C) (10, 11)

(D) (11, 10)

(E) (13, 4)

3. Line *M* is $y = 3x + 10$. Line *N* is $2y = 5x − 6$. Line *P* has a *y*-intercept of 6, and the point (6, 4) lies on line *P*.

Quantity A	**Quantity B**
The measure of the largest angle created by the intersection of line *M* and line *N*	The measure of the largest angle created by the intersection of line *M* and line *P*

9

4.

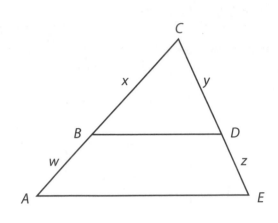

BD is parallel to AE.

Quantity A	**Quantity B**
xz	wy

5.

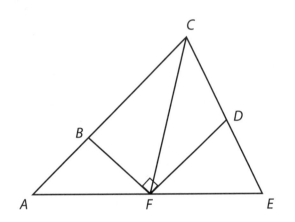

F is the midpoint of AE, and D is the midpoint of CE.

Which of the following statements MUST be true?

Indicate all such statements.

- [A] FD is parallel to AC.
- [B] The area of triangle DEF equals the area of triangle CDF.
- [C] The area of triangle ABF is less than the area of triangle DEF.
- [D] Angle AFB equals angle BFC.
- [E] The area of triangle ACE equals AC × BF.

MANHATTAN
PREP

9

6.

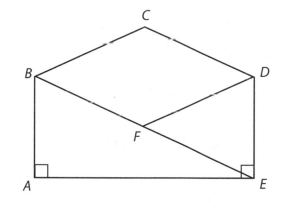

AB = DE, *BC = CD*, *BE* is parallel to *CD*, and *BC* is parallel to *DF*.

Quantity A

The area of triangle *ABE*

Quantity B

The area of quadrilateral *BCDF*

7.

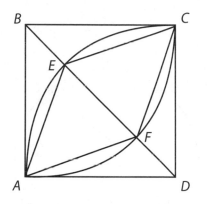

In the figure above, *ABCD* is a square with sides equal to 1, *AFC* is an arc of a circle centered at *B*, and *AEC* is an arc of a circle centered at *D*. What is the area of rhombus *AECF*?

(A) $2 - \sqrt{2}$

(B) $\sqrt{2} - 1$

(C) $\sqrt{2}\left(2 - \sqrt{2}\right)$

(D) $\sqrt{2}$

(E) $1 + \sqrt{2}$

9

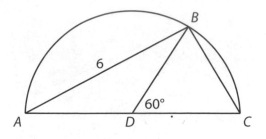

8. Triangle *ABC* is inscribed in a semicircle centered at *D*. What is the area of triangle *ABC*?

(A) $\dfrac{12}{\sqrt{3}}$

(B) $6\sqrt{3}$

(C) 12

(D) $12\sqrt{3}$

(E) $18\sqrt{3}$

9.

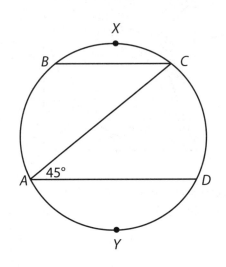

The circle above has radius 8, and *AD* is parallel to *BC*. If the length of arc *AYD* is twice the length of arc *BXC*, what is the length of arc *BXC*?

(A) 2π

(B) $\dfrac{8\pi}{3}$

(C) 3π

(D) 4π

(E) $\dfrac{16\pi}{3}$

10.

Quantity A	**Quantity B**
The volume of a right circular cylinder with radius and height each equal to 3	84

11.

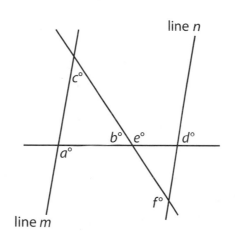

Lines *m* and *n* are parallel.

Considering each choice separately, having values for which of the following variables or pairs of variables would be sufficient to determine the measure of angle *a*?

Indicate <u>all</u> such values.

A   *b*

B   *c*

C   *d*

D   *b* and *c*

E   *c* and *e*

F   *b* and *f*

G   *c* and *f*

9

12.

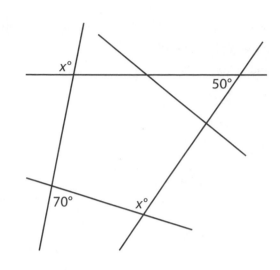

In the figure above, what is x?

13.

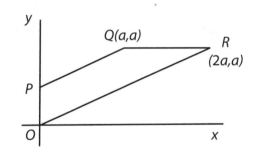

Trapezoid *OPQR* has one vertex at the origin. What is the area of *OPQR*?

(A) $\dfrac{a^2}{4}$

(B) $\dfrac{a^2}{2}$

(C) $\dfrac{3a^2}{4}$

(D) $\dfrac{3a^2}{2}$

(E) $2a^2$

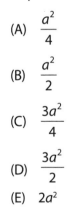

MANHATTAN
PREP

14. Perpendicular lines m and n intersect at point (a, b), where $a > b > 0$. The slope of line m is between 0 and 1. Which of the following statements MUST be true?

Indicate <u>all</u> such statements.

- [A] The x-intercept of line m is positive.
- [B] The y-intercept of line m is negative.
- [C] The x-intercept of line n is positive.
- [D] The y-intercept of line n is negative.
- [E] The product of the x- and y-intercepts of line m is not positive.
- [F] The sum of the x-intercepts of lines m and n is positive.

15.

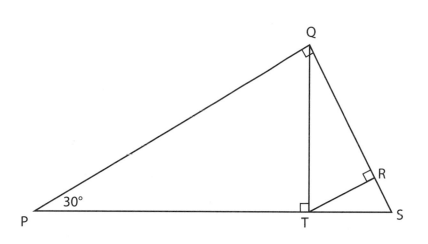

If $PQ = 1$, what is the length of RS?

(A) $\dfrac{1}{12}$

(B) $\dfrac{\sqrt{3}}{12}$

(C) $\dfrac{1}{6}$

(D) $\dfrac{2}{3\sqrt{3}}$

(E) $\dfrac{2}{\sqrt{12}}$

16. If the length of one side of a regular hexagon (all sides and angles equal) is 8, what is the area of the hexagon?

    (A) 48

    (B) $36\sqrt{3}$

    (C) $48\sqrt{2}$

    (D) $96\sqrt{3}$

    (E) $128\sqrt{2}$

17. The average measure of the interior angles of an n-sided polygon is divisible by 10. For which values of n could this be true?

    Indicate <u>all</u> such values.

    | A | 4 |
    | B | 5 |
    | C | 6 |
    | D | 8 |
    | E | 9 |
    | F | 10 |

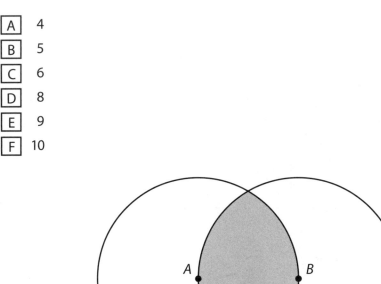

18. In the figure above, A and B are the centers of the two circles. If each circle has radius x, what is the area of the shaded region?

    (A) $\dfrac{\left(2\pi - \sqrt{3}\right)x^2}{6}$

    (D) $\dfrac{\left(4\pi - \sqrt{3}\right)x^2}{6}$

    (B) $\dfrac{\left(4\pi - 3\sqrt{3}\right)x^2}{12}$

    (E) $\dfrac{\left(6\pi - 1\right)x^2}{6}$

    (C) $\dfrac{\left(4\pi - 3\sqrt{3}\right)x^2}{6}$

19. In the *xy*-plane, line *n* is a line that passes through the origin.

Which of the following statements individually provide(s) sufficient additional information to determine whether the slope of line *n* is greater than 1?

Indicate all such statements.

A Line *n* does not pass through any point (a, b) where a and b are positive and $a > b$.

B Line *m* is perpendicular to line *n* and has a slope of -1.

C Line *n* passes through the point (c, $d+1$) where c and d are consecutive integers and $c > d$.

20.

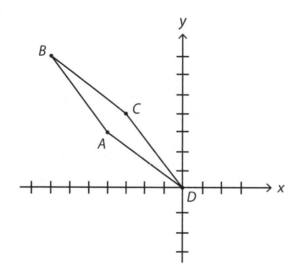

Parallelogram *ABCD* lies in the *xy*-plane, as shown in the figure above. The coordinates of point *C* are $(-3, 4)$ and the coordinates of point *B* are $(-7, 7)$. What is the area of the parallelogram?

(A) 1

(B) $2\sqrt{7}$

(C) 7

(D) 8

(E) $7\sqrt{2}$

Hard Practice Question Solutions

1. 192: Using the formula for the surface area of a cube (Area = $6s^2$), you can find the surface area by simply finding the length of one of the sides of the cube.

Flipping the cube so that the bottom of it is visible (and noting that this bottom surface is a square), you can see that line segment *AB* divides the square into two equal 45–45–90 triangles. Label one of the sides *s*:

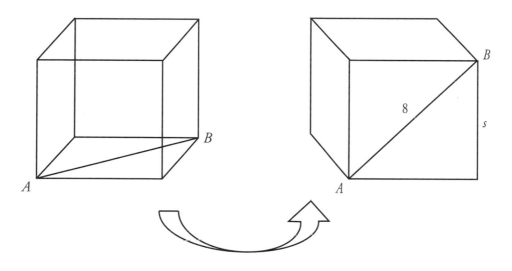

Applying the rule that the sides of a 45–45–90 triangle are in the proportion $1:1:\sqrt{2}$, within a square these dimensions are $s:s:s\sqrt{2}$, where *s* is the side length. If $s\sqrt{2} = 8$, then $s = \dfrac{8}{\sqrt{2}}$.

Therefore, the area of the bottom square is $\left(\dfrac{8}{\sqrt{2}}\right)^2 = \dfrac{64}{2} = 32$. and the surface area of the entire cube is $32 \times 6 = 192$.

2. (C): Since point *A* is at the origin (0, 0) and point *B* is at (3, 4), you can determine that $AB = 5$ by applying the distance formula (Pythagorean theorem):

$$\text{Distance} = \sqrt{\left(\text{Change in } x \text{ coordinates}\right)^2 + \left(\text{Change in } y \text{ coordinates}\right)^2}$$

In this case, $\text{Distance} = \sqrt{(3-0)^2 + (4-0)^2} = \sqrt{9+16} = \sqrt{25} = 5$. (You could also note that *AB* forms the hypotenuse of a 3–4–5 right triangle, by filling in a line segment from *B* to the *x*-axis.)

Since $AB = 5$, you know that $BC = 2(5) = 10$. Now you need to determine which of the listed points are *not* 10 units away from (3, 4).

Choice (E) is the easiest to eliminate, as you can simply add 10 the *x* value of point *B* perpendicular to arrive at the location of *C*. That line segment will be 10 units long.

9

To handle the other choices, you need to calculate their distances from (3, 4). Again, use the distance formula. For answer choice (A): $\sqrt{\left(3-(-5)\right)^2 + \left(4-(-2)\right)^2} = \sqrt{8^2+6^2} = \sqrt{64+36} = \sqrt{100} = 10$. (Note: this is a 6–8–10 right triangle. Recognizing this pattern saves a lot of calculation time!)

For answer choice (B): $\sqrt{(3-9)^2 + (4-12)^2} = \sqrt{6^2+8^2} = \sqrt{36+64} = \sqrt{100} = 10$. (Note: this also is a 6–8–10 right triangle!)

For answer choice (C): $\sqrt{(3-10)^2 + (4-11)^2} = \sqrt{7^2+7^2} = \sqrt{49+49} = \sqrt{98} = 7\sqrt{2}$. You can now use the on-screen calculator to determine that $7\sqrt{2}$ is larger than 10, and thus choice (C) is the correct answer.

For choice (D): $\sqrt{(3-11)^2 + (4-10)^2} = \sqrt{8^2+6^2} = \sqrt{64+36} = \sqrt{100} = 10$. (Note: this is the same 6–8–10 triangle as in choice (B), but the legs have been switched!)

3. **(A):** The measure of the angles created at the intersection of any two lines is a function of the relative slopes of the lines. Since you are given enough information to solve for the slope of each of the lines involved, you can eliminate choice (D) immediately—you have enough information for a solution.

The slopes of lines M and N can be calculated directly since you are provided with equations that describe the lines. In the generic equation $y = mx + b$, m is the slope of the line and b is the y-intercept. Thus, the slope of M is 3 and the slope of N is $\dfrac{5}{2}$ (you obtain the slope of line N by dividing both sides of the equation for N by 2). Since you know that line P contains the points (0, 6) and (6, 4), you can compute the slope of the line as follows:

$$\text{Slope } \frac{\Delta y}{\Delta x} = \frac{(6-4)}{(0-6)} = -\frac{1}{3}$$

The slope of line P is the negative reciprocal of the slope of line M; *by definition this means that the lines are perpendicular.* It follows that every angle created by the intersection of lines M and P must be 90°.

Since lines M and N are *not* perpendicular or parallel, you know that the intersection creates two angles of less than 90° and two angles of greater than 90°. Thus, **Quantity A is greater.**

4. **(C):** Because *BD* is parallel to *AE*, angle *CBD* is equal to angle *CAE*, and angle *BDC* is equal to angle *AEC*. This implies that triangles *BCD* and *ACE* are similar. Similar triangles have the property that ratios of the lengths of corresponding sides are equal. Consider the left sides: the length of the left side of triangle *BCD* is *x*, whereas the length of the left side of triangle *ACE* is *x* + *w*. Likewise, the right sides have lengths *y* and *y* + *z*, respectively. Therefore:

$$\frac{x}{x+w} = \frac{y}{y+z}$$

$$xy + xz = xy + wy \qquad \text{Cross-multiply.}$$

$$xz = wy$$

Thus, **the two quantities are equal**.

5. **(A), (B),** and **(E):** Choice (A): Because *DE* is $\frac{1}{2}$ of *CE* and *FE* is $\frac{1}{2}$ of *AE* (i.e., corresponding sides have proportional lengths), and angle *DEF* is shared between the two triangles, you can see that triangles *ACE* and *FDE* must be similar. Similar triangles have the further property that corresponding angles are of equal measure. Thus, for example, angle *DFE* equals angle *CAE*, and so *FD* is parallel to *AC*.

Choice (B): Looking at the two smaller triangles in the right half of the figure, you can see that triangle *CDF* and triangle *DEF* have collinear and equal "bases" (*CD* and *DE*), and share their third vertex (*F*), which is some fixed distance away from *CE*. Because *CE* is comprised of bases *CD* and *DE* of triangles *CDF* and *DEF*, respectively, the two triangles have the same height. Because *CDF* and *DEF* have equal bases and the same height, they must have the same area. (For a similar reason, triangles *ACF* and *FCE* must have equal areas; more on that later.)

Choices (C) and (D) need not be true. The figure has been redrawn below so as to serve as a counter-example to both. In general, trying to "deform" the figure while remaining within the specified constraints is an effective way to discover which statements remain true and which do not.

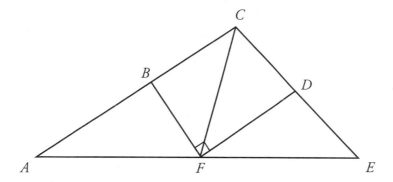

Choice (E): Because triangles *ACF* and *FCE* must have equal areas as indicated above, you can see that the area of triangle *ACE* must be twice that of triangle *ACF*. Note that *FD* is parallel to *AC* due to (true) choice (A), and *BF* is perpendicular to *FD*. Therefore, *BF* must be perpendicular to *AC* as well. Put differently, *AC* can be regarded as the base, and *BF* the height, of triangle *ACF*. The area of triangle *ACF* equals $\frac{1}{2}$ times *AC* × *BF*. The area of triangle *ACE*, which is twice that of *ACF*, must therefore equal *AC* × *BF*.

9

6. **(C)**: Because of the various parallel and equal length constraints, you can see that quadrilateral *BCDF* is a rhombus with side lengths equal to half diagonal BE. In fact, the whole shape can be split into 10 identical right triangles, as shown:

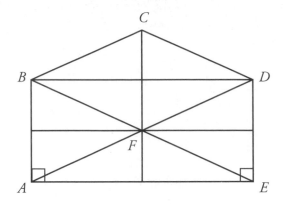

Quantity A	**Quantity B**
The area of triangle *ABE*	The area of quadrilateral *BCDF*
= 4 small triangles	= 4 small triangles

Therefore, **the two quantities are equal**.

7. **(B)**: The area of a rhombus is equal to $\frac{1}{2}$ times the product of its diagonals. One diagonal of *AECF* is *AC*, which is also a diagonal of the square, and thus has length $\sqrt{2}$. (You can use either the Pythagorean theorem or the 45–45–90 triangle rule to prove this.) The length of the other diagonal, *EF*, can be determined as follows: both *BF* and *DE* are radii of quarter-circles, each of which has a side on the square that is also a radius. The sides of the square equal 1, so *BF* and *DE* must equal 1. Therefore, *BF* + *DE* = 2. Notice that *BF* and *DE* also lie along the other diagonal of the square, *BD*. The length of *BD* is equal to $\sqrt{2}$. The reason *BF* + *DE* is greater than *BD* is that *BF* and *DE* overlap; the length of the overlap *EF* is counted twice. Thus, you can find the length of *EF* by subtracting the length of *BD* from the sum of *BF* and *DE*: $EF = 2 - \sqrt{2}$. Finally, you compute the area of *AECF* as follows:

$$\text{Area} = \frac{1}{2}(AC)(EF) = \frac{1}{2}\left(\sqrt{2}\right)\left(2 - \sqrt{2}\right) = \frac{1}{2}\left(2\sqrt{2} - 2\right) = \sqrt{2} - 1$$

An alternative is to eliminate answer choices based on estimation. The area of *AECF* appears to be around one-half of the area of the square, which equals 1. Thus, you would expect the value of the answer to be around 0.5. Seen in that light, only choices (A) and (B) make sense.

8. **(B):** You can redraw the figure, adding any information you can infer:

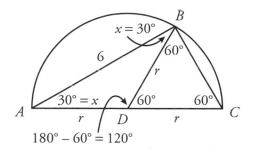

Any triangle inscribed in a semi-circle is a right triangle. Each segment from D to a point on the circle is a radius, so $AD = CD = BD = r$. Triangle ABD is an isoceles triangle, so the two angles marked x are equal and $2x + 120 = 180$, so $x = 30$. Thus, ABC is a 30–60–90 triangle, and BCD is an equilateral triangle, so BC also equals r.

By using the Pythagorean theorem on ABC, you find:

$$6^2 + r^2 = (2r)^2$$
$$36 + r^2 = 4r^2$$
$$36 = 3r^2$$
$$12 = r^2$$
$$r = \sqrt{12} = 2\sqrt{3}$$

The area of $ABC = \dfrac{1}{2}(6)\left(2\sqrt{3}\right) = 6\sqrt{3}$.

9. **(B):** Because AD is parallel to BC, the measure of angle ACB is also 45°. Angles CAD and ACB are both inscribed angles of the circle. The measures of the corresponding central angles are twice 45°, or 90° each. Therefore, taken together, minor arcs AB and CD make up 180° of the entire circle, leaving 180° for arcs BXC and AYD. Because arc AYD is twice the length of arc BXC, arc BXC must correspond to a 60° central angle and arc AYD to a 120° central angle. Therefore, arc BXC is $\dfrac{60}{360} = \dfrac{1}{6}$ of the entire circumference of the circle, which equals $2\pi r = 16\pi$. The length of arc BXC is thus $\dfrac{16\pi}{6} = \dfrac{8\pi}{3}$.

10. **(A):** The volume of a right circular cylinder is given by the formula $V = \pi r^2 h$. In this case, the volume equals $\pi(3^2)(3) = 27\pi$. Using the approximate value of $\pi = 3.14$ on the GRE calculator, the volume is computed as $V = 3.14 \times 27 = 84.78$, which is greater than 84. (Note that since π is slightly larger than 3.14, the volume will be slightly larger than 84.78.)

9

11. **(C), (D), (E),** and **(F):** Refer to the figure below, in which some of the angle labels have been repli-
cated. This updated figure is based on the various angular equalities associated with parallel lines (lines
m and *n*) being intersected by a transversal:

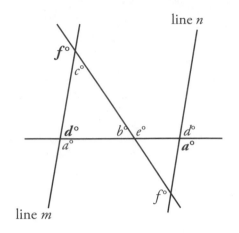

It can be seen that angles *b* and *c* individually have no relation to *a*, but they are "remote interior angles"
in a triangle of which *a* is an exterior angle. Thus, by the exterior angle rule, the measure of *a* is equal
to the sum of the measures of *b* and *c*. (This is true because $a + d = 180°$, and $b + c + d = 180°$, so $a = b + c$.)
Thus, knowing the values of *b* and *c* is sufficient to find *a*, so choice (D) is correct.

It can also be seen from the figure that *a* and *d*, *b* and *e*, and *c* and *f* are pairs of supplementary angles
(they sum to 180°). In other words, knowing one angle's value provides the value of the other. Thus, *d*
is sufficient to find *a*. Also, knowing *c* and *e* is sufficient to find *a* (because *e* is sufficient to find *b*), and
knowing *b* and *f* is sufficient (because *f* is sufficient to find *c*). Hence, choices (C), (E), and (F) are correct.

12. **100:** Some additional angle measures have been entered into the figure below:

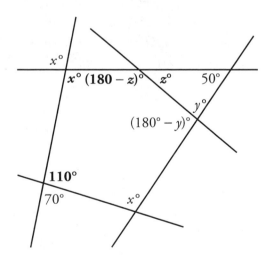

The polygon in the center of the figure is a pentagon. The sum of the interior angles of an *n*-sided
polygon is given by $(n - 2) \times 180°$. For a pentagon, this yields $(5 - 2) \times 180° = 540°$.

MANHATTAN
PREP

From the sum of the angles in the pentagon: $x + (180 - z) + (180 - y) + x + 110 = 540$, or $2x = 70 + y + z$.
From the sum of the angles in the triangle at the upper right of the figure: $50 + y + z = 180$, so $y + z = 130$.
Thus, $2x = 70 + 130 = 200$, so $x = 100$.

13. **(C):** Consider the figure below, which has additional lines, labels, and coordinates filled in:

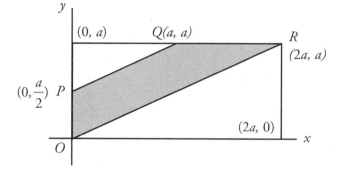

The area of trapezoid *OPQR* can be found by subtracting the areas of the unshaded right triangles from the area of rectangle shown. (This allows you to arrive at the value of the shaded area in the figure, which is the original trapezoid.) Because *OPQR* is a trapezoid, *PQ* is parallel to *OR* and has

a slope equal to $\dfrac{a}{2a} = \dfrac{1}{2}$. The *y*-coordinate of *P* must therefore equal $\dfrac{a}{2}$. The area of the rectangle

is $2a \times a = 2a^2$, the area of the top triangle is $\dfrac{1}{2}\left(\dfrac{a}{2}\right)(a) = \dfrac{a^2}{4}$, and the area of the bottom triangle is

$\dfrac{1}{2}(2a)(a) = a^2$. Thus, the area of *OPQR* is $2a^2 - \dfrac{a^2}{4} - a^2 = \dfrac{3a^2}{4}$.

14. **(C)** and **(E):** Consider the figures below, which illustrate various arrangements of the lines that satisfy the given constraints. It can be seen that the *x*- and *y*-intercepts of line *n* will always be positive. Those of line *m* can be zero, positive, or negative; when both intercepts are non-zero, the two intercepts have opposite signs. That is why their product has to be negative. Lastly, even though it first appears that the *x*-intercept of line *n* would always be farther from zero than the *x*-intercept of line *m*, the last figure illustrates that this need not always be the case. Thus, choice (F) is not necessarily true:

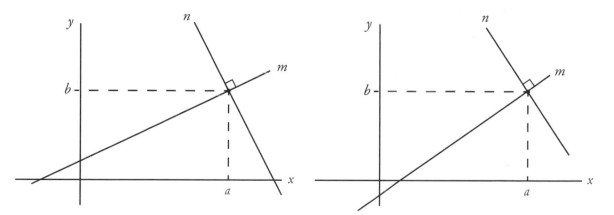

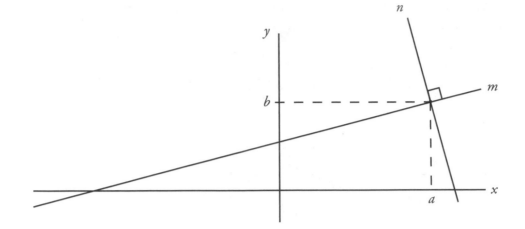

15. (B): Note that every triangle in this figure is a 30–60–90 triangle, inferred from the given angles. All must have sides in the proportion $1 : \sqrt{3} : 2$:

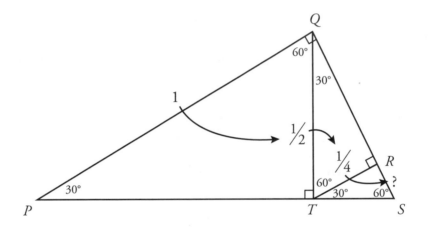

If $PQ = 1$, $QT = 1/2$. If $QT = 1/2$, $RT = 1/4$. If RT is the long leg in triangle RST, $RT = x\sqrt{3} = 1/4$ and the short leg $RS = 1x$.

$$x = \frac{\frac{1}{4}}{\sqrt{3}} \times \frac{\sqrt{3}}{\sqrt{3}} = \frac{\sqrt{3}}{12}, \text{ so } RS = \frac{\sqrt{3}}{12}.$$

16. (D): You can start by drawing a regular hexagon. Since the sum of the interior angles of an *n*-sided polygon must equal $(n - 2) \times 180$, the sum of the angles will equal $(6 - 2) \times 180 = 720$ and each angle will equal 120. You can divide the hexagon into a rectangular piece and four right triangles as follows:

MANHATTAN
PREP

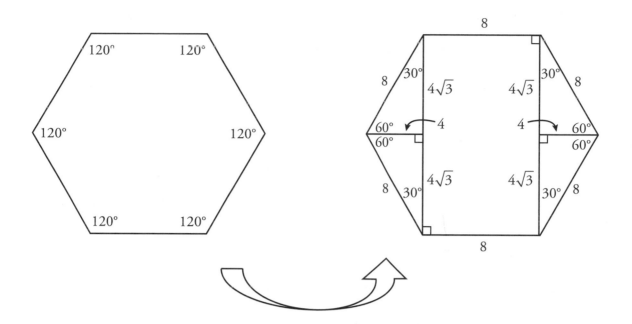

From this diagram you can determine that the rectangle has a width of 8 and the four right triangles have hypotenuses of length 8. Because they are 30–60–90 triangles, the sides must be in the ratio of $1 : \sqrt{3} : 2$, so the short legs of the right triangles equal 4 and the long legs equal $4\sqrt{3}$. Thus, the rectangle has a height of $2\left(4\sqrt{3}\right) = 8\sqrt{3}$ and, furthermore, an area of $8 \times 8\sqrt{3} = 64\sqrt{3}$.

Each of the four right triangles has a base of 4 and a height of $4\sqrt{3}$, so the area of each is $\frac{1}{2}(4)\left(4\sqrt{3}\right) = 8\sqrt{3}$, and since there are four of them, they contribute $4\left(8\sqrt{3}\right) = 32\sqrt{3}$ to the area of the hexagon.

Adding the area of the rectangle to that of the four right triangles, you get a total area for the hexagon of $64\sqrt{3} + 32\sqrt{3} = 96\sqrt{3}$.

Note also that the hexagon could be divided into six equal equilateral triangles, each with a base of 8 and a height of $4\sqrt{3}$. The area of each such equilateral triangle equals $\frac{1}{2}(8)\left(4\sqrt{3}\right) = 16\sqrt{3}$, and $6 \times 16\sqrt{3} = 96\sqrt{3}$.

9

17. **(A), (C),** and **(E):** Since the sum of the interior angles of an n-sided polygon must equal $(n-2) \times 180°$, the average of the angles will equal: $\dfrac{(n-2) \times 180°}{n} = \dfrac{180°n - 360°}{n} = 180° - \dfrac{360°}{n}$.

Since 180 is divisible by 10, you need only evaluate whether $\dfrac{360}{n}$ is divisible by 10 for each answer choice:

$\boxed{A}$ $\dfrac{360}{4} = 90$, which is divisible by 10. In other words, 4-sided polygons will have an average angle of $180° - 90° = 90°$, which **is divisible by 10.**

$\boxed{B}$ $\dfrac{360}{5} = 72$, which is NOT divisible by 10. In other words, 5-sided polygons will have an average angle of $180° - 72° = 108°$, which is NOT divisible by 10.

$\boxed{C}$ $\dfrac{360}{6} = 60$, which is divisible by 10. In other words, 6-sided polygons will have an average angle of $180° - 60° = 120°$, which **is divisible by 10.**

$\boxed{D}$ $\dfrac{360}{8} = 45$, which is NOT divisible by 10. In other words, 8-sided polygons will have an average angle of $180° - 45° = 135°$, which is NOT divisible by 10.

$\boxed{E}$ $\dfrac{360}{9} = 40$, which is divisible by 10. In other words, 9-sided polygons will have an average angle of $180° - 40° = 140°$, which **is divisible by 10.**

$\boxed{F}$ $\dfrac{360}{10} = 36$, which is NOT divisible by 10. In other words, 10-sided polygons will have an average angle of $180° - 36° = 144°$, which is NOT divisible by 10.

18. **(C):** The easiest way to solve this problem is to add a few lines to the diagram:

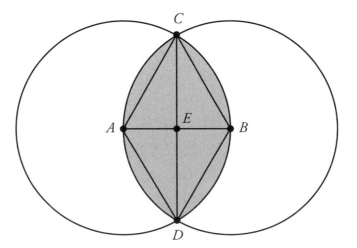

9

Because AB, AC, AD, BC, and BD are all radii of one of the circles, they are of equal length (all equal to x) and form two equilateral triangles: ABC and ABD. Therefore, angles ACB and ADB are 60° each, and angles CAD and CBD each equal 120°. Line segment CD bisects angles ACB and ADB and is perpendicular to line segment AB. Therefore, triangles ACE, ADE, BCE, and BDE are all 30–60–90 triangles.

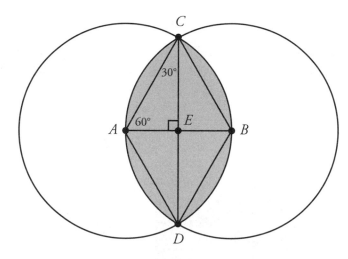

Because angle $CAD = 120°$, it intercepts an arc equal to $\dfrac{1}{3}$ of the area of circle A. The area of circle A is given by πx^2, so the area of the sector intercepted by that angle is $\dfrac{\pi x^2}{3}$. Similarly, the area of the arc intercepted by angle CBD is $\dfrac{\pi x^2}{3}$. Adding these together, you get $\dfrac{2\pi x^2}{3}$. However, this measure double counts the four 30–60–90 triangles in the middle of the region. Therefore, you must subtract out their areas.

Each of the 30–60–90 triangles has a hypotenuse of x and a short leg of $\dfrac{x}{2}$. Using the proportion $1 : \sqrt{3} : 2$ for the sides of a 30-60-90 triangle, the long legs of these four triangles equal $\dfrac{x}{\sqrt{3}} = \dfrac{x\sqrt{3}}{3}$.

Therefore the area of each triangle equals $\dfrac{1}{2}bh = \dfrac{1}{2}\left(\dfrac{x\sqrt{3}}{2}\right)\left(\dfrac{x}{2}\right) = \dfrac{x^2\sqrt{3}}{8}$. Since there are four of them,

the total area of the 30–60–90 triangles is $\dfrac{4x^2\sqrt{3}}{8} = \dfrac{x^2\sqrt{3}}{2}$.

Therefore, the total area of the shaded region equals: $\dfrac{2\pi x^2}{3} - \dfrac{x^2\sqrt{3}}{2} = \dfrac{4\pi x^2 - 3\sqrt{3}x^2}{6} = \dfrac{\left(4\pi - 3\sqrt{3}\right)x^2}{6}$.

19. **(B)** and **(C)**: Choice (A) tells you that line n does not pass through any point that has a larger x-coordinate than its y-coordinate. Because line n passes through the origin, this means the line does not have a slope of $\dfrac{b}{a}$, where $a > b$. In other words, line n does not have a positive slope of *less* than 1. This does not answer the question, because line n could still have a slope of *exactly* 1, or a slope *greater than* 1, or a *negative* slope, or a 0 slope.

Choice (B), however, answers the question, because the slope of line n must equal the negative recipro-cal of perpendicular line m, which is -1. Thus, line n has a slope of $-\left(\dfrac{1}{-1}\right) = 1$.

Choice (C) also answers the question: if c and d are consecutive integers and c is larger than d, then $c = d + 1$. Thus, line n passes through the point (c, c), and thus has a slope of $\dfrac{c}{c} = 1$. This is true even if c is negative.

20. **(C):** Perhaps the easiest way to solve this problem is to draw a rectangle around the parallelogram, find its area, and subtract out the area of the triangles that emerge around the parallelogram, within the rectangle (but that are not part of the parallelogram):

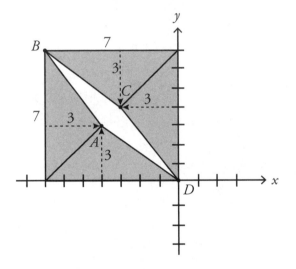

Since $ABCD$ is a parallelogram, line segments AB and CD have the same length and the same slope. Therefore, in the diagram above, point A is at $(-4, 3)$. The square has an area of $7 \times 7 = 49$. By drawing carefully and exploiting similar triangles created by various parallel lines, you can label the height of each triangle 3, and each base 7. Each triangle has area $\dfrac{1}{2}bh = \dfrac{1}{2}(7)(3) = \dfrac{21}{2}$. Therefore, the area of par-allelogram $ABCD$ equals $49 - 4\left(\dfrac{21}{2}\right) = 49 - 42 = 7$.

Although the GRE does not require knowledge of this formula, a direct way to calculate the area of a rhombus requires only the diagonals of the rhombus, which are of length $\sqrt{7^2 + 7^2} = 7\sqrt{2}$ and $\sqrt{1^2 + 1^2} = \sqrt{2}$. Using the formula for the area of a rhombus, $\dfrac{d_1 \times d_2}{2}$, you get $\dfrac{7\sqrt{2}}{2} \times \sqrt{2} = 7$.

STUDY ANYWHERE!
WITH MANHATTAN PREP'S GRE FLASH CARDS

coterie

(noun)

COH-ter-ee

587

Definition: Close or exclusive group, clique

Usage: The pop star never traveled anywhere without a **coterie** of assistants and managers.

Related Words: *Cabal* (conspiracy, group of people who plot), *Entourage* (group of attendants)

More Info: In French, a *coterie* was a group of tenant farmers.

With our flashcards you can study both math and verbal concepts on the go!

Both our 500 Essential Words and a 500 Advanced Words cards go above and beyond providing abstract, out-of-context definitions. Complete with definitions, example sentences, pronunciations, and related words, this two-volume set comprises the most comprehensive vocabulary study tool on the market.

Our GRE Math Flash Cards provide practical exposure to the basic math concepts tested on the GRE.

Designed to be user-friendly for all students, these cards include easy-to-follow explanations of math concepts that promise to enhance comprehension and build fundamental skills.

For the revised GRE

MANHATTAN PREP

GRE® FLASH CARDS

500 Math Flash Cards

✓ Designed specifically for the math question types found on the revised GRE

✓ Cards cover all tested content and include clear, efficient explanations

✓ Want Verbal? Check out our flash card sets 500 Essential Words & 500 Advanced Words

*GRE is a registered trademark of the Educational Testing Service (ETS), which neither sponsors nor endorses this test product.

NEED MORE THAN BOOKS ALONE?

TRY OUR GUIDED SELF-STUDY PROGRAM!

With over 27 hours of recorded video lessons, Guided Self-Study is a perfect fit for self-motivated individuals who want full access to all of Manhattan Prep's materials.

Armed with our syllabus and online resources suite, you can get more out of your books. This program is a great fit for students operating under a tight deadline or rigid schedule who may not have the time to take a live prep course.

Check it out at manhattanprep.com/gre/gre-self-study.cfm